NEYLAND
LIFE OF A STADIUM

is presented to

_____

with all best wishes.

"Give Him Six!"

John Ward
John Ward

Robin Hood
Robin Hood

Barry Parker
Barry Parker

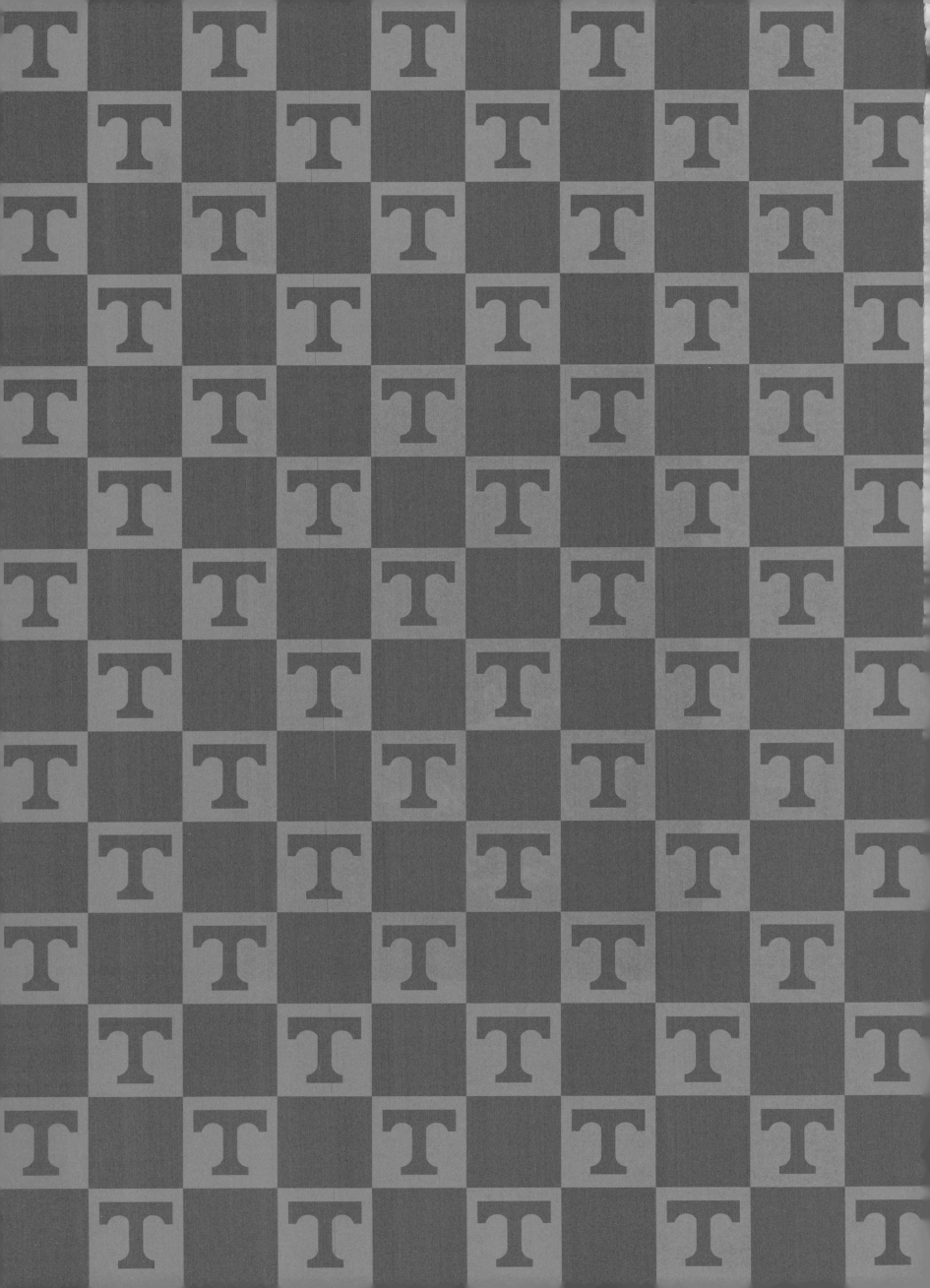

This book is made possible
through the generous support of our sponsors:

Frank E. Neal & Co.

NEYLAND

LIFE OF A STADIUM

by BARRY PARKER & ROBIN HOOD
Introduction by JOHN WARD

PARKER HOOD
PRESS

NEYLAND: *Life Of A Stadium*

COPYRIGHT © 2000 BY PARKER HOOD PRESS, INC.
TEXT COPYRIGHT © 2000 by Barry Parker
PHOTOGRAPHS COPYRIGHT © 2000 by Robin Hood
INTRODUCTION COPYRIGHT © 2000 by John Ward

Published by:
Parker Hood Press, Inc., 340 Crest Terrace Drive, Chattanooga, TN
37404; phone: 800/563-1235

Library of Congress Control Number: 00-091962
ISBN 0-9645704-7-5

Grateful acknowledgment for the use of photographs is made
to the following:
University of Tennessee Athletic Archives, University of Tennessee
Special Collections, McClung Historical Collection, University of
Tennessee Music Department, Knoxville News-Sentinel, Thompson
Photo Products, Collection of Dr. Andrew Kozar, Collection of
Arthur Fields and Collection of Trey White, and photographers Joe
Howell, Michael Patrick, Marvin Dockery and Scott West. All
contributed photographs are copyrighted to the individual
photographer. *Sports Illustrated* covers on p.44, © 1967 Walter
Iooss, Jr.; and p.59, © 1999 Al Tielemans, used by permission of
Sports Illustrated.

Designed by Robertson Design, Inc., Brentwood, Tennessee
Separations by Color Systems, Inc., Nashville, Tennessee
Printed in Hong Kong through C & C Offset Printing Co., Inc.

FIRST EDITION
Second Printing: March 2001

NEYLAND
LIFE OF A STADIUM

VOLS

ACKNOWLEDGMENTS

The authors wish to thank those who provided assistance throughout the project, and in particular:

Tom Mattingly, whose encyclopedic knowledge of Vol football facts and lore and writings on the subject he loves proved invaluable, and whose time and help are deeply appreciated;
Bud Ford, who opened the archives to us and graciously fulfilled our many requests;
Haywood Harris, who gave us the keys to the stadium — from the locker room to the sidelines to the press box;
Mike Hamilton, who worked closely and enthusiastically with us to spread the word about the book through the UT network;
Mitch Barnhart, former senior associate athletic director, who supported the project from the start;
Dr. Andrew Kozar, who shared his colorful Vol memorabilia and reminiscences with us;
Judy Dooley and John Martin, who helped us relate the history of the Pride of the Southland Marching Band, and Martha Masengill, who did the same for the cheer-leading squad;
Bob Campbell, who gave us a ground view of the field he and his staff lovingly tend;
Earl and Martha Hudson, who proudly prepared Smokey VIII for his cover photograph;
Nick Myers, Sarah Huff and Bob Hillhouse of UT Photo Services for their diligent retrieval of negatives and printing of Vol football photos from their archives;
Steve Cotham and Sally Polhemus of Knox County Public Library System's McClung Historical Collection for their help locating photographs;
Nick Wyman and Bill Eigelsbach of UT Special Collections, who helped find many of the rare illustrations and photographs of early teams and stadium scenes;
Harry Moskos, editor of the *Knoxville News-Sentinel*, who opened the newspaper's photo archives to our research;
Joe Howell and Michael Patrick, *Knoxville News-Sentinel* photographers, who contributed photographs from their files;
Marvin Dockery and Scott West, Knoxville freelance photographers, who contributed classic game-day aerial photographs of Neyland Stadium;
Thompson Photo Product for vintage UT football images by pioneer photographer James E. Thompson, who created a classic photographic record of East Tennessee in a 60-year career begun in 1902;
Bud Fields, who placed his life-long collection of Vol photographs, and his knowledgeable commentary, at our disposal;
Avid fan Trey White, who shared his collection of memorabilia with us;
Neal O'Steen, whose colorful research and text for booklets on Neyland Stadium's history paved the way for our account;
Those who have written colorfully about Vol football recently including Ward Gossett (VOLUNTEERS HANDBOOK: *Stories, Stats and Stuff About Tennessee Football*), Tom Mattingly (TENNESSEE FOOTBALL: *The Peyton Manning Years*), Alan Ross (BIG ORANGE WISDOM); Tim Cohane's article: "Robert Neyland: The Gridiron General," and the Volunteer football program's annual compendium of information;
Our friends, Jed Mescon and Bill Stiles, who planted the idea for the book, and Dr. Joe Parker, who helped nurture it;
Our colleagues at Robertson Design—John Robertson, Jeff Carroll and John Schaeffer— who infused this work with remarkable vision, creativity and devotion;
And to LeNet and Peggy for their abiding and loving support.

Barry Parker and Robin Hood

A PERFECT PLACE by John Ward

In my opinion, there's no more beautiful place in the country to watch the game of college football than Neyland Stadium. There are stadiums with wonderful, wonderful histories, but none I know has achieved Neyland's perfect form through so many building programs, as if shaped by a master plan.

Like other East Tennesseans, my love affair with the stadium began when I was a youngster. It occurred in the 1940s when Shields-Watkins Field, as it was then called, consisted of east and west stands and bleachers in the end zones. I was 14 and a member of a Knoxville Boy Scout troop. Five of us were chosen to usher Tennessee home games, and that was the highlight of my early years. No recognition I've since received has been sweeter than that honor.

Less than a decade later, I was working as a young reporter for the *Knoxville Journal* when, on a cold, rainy afternoon when none of the veteran staff wanted to cover UT's football practice, they sent me. I was thrilled. When I got to the field, General Robert Neyland, then the university's athletic director and former football coach, was parking his car. "Ward," he said, "come and sit with me." I was amazed he knew my name and searched for something reasonable to ask him. Finally, I said: "General, I've heard people pronounce your name NAY-land and KNEE-land. What do you say?" He answered: "Where I

come from, they say KNEE-land." And that's what I've called him and the stadium since, though people still try to correct me.

The General was more than a coaching legend; he was an engineer trained at West Point and MIT, and he was passionately involved in the physical development of the stadium. During his tenure as coach and athletic director, he oversaw three expansion projects, and a fourth was under way when he died. Yet, in his grandest vision, could he have foreseen what the field would one day be: a majestic coliseum seating nearly 105,000, making it one of the great sports venues on earth? I don't know, but this I do: he set in motion the events that made it possible.

In 1957, when the horseshoe-shaped field could seat 46,000, I became the public address announcer, a job I held for eight years. One game I'll never forget. We were playing LSU in 1959 when the Tigers were undefeated and the defending national champion. Surprisingly, we were ahead. After a fourth-quarter LSU touchdown made the score 14-13, they elected to go for a two-point conversion and victory.

Billy Cannon, their great back, ran off right tackle and was stopped at the goal line. I saw the referee on the east side come in to the play and prepare to signal a touchdown when I announced over the PA system, rather emphatically: "Cannon carries. He did NOT make it." At that instant, it seems to me, the official reversed himself and put his hands down, indicating no score. "You won the game! You won the game!" my spotter, a fraternity brother, whispered excitedly to me. Did I influence the call? I don't know myself, but I do know I was more cheerleader than unbiased announcer that day, and "The

Stop" of Billy Cannon entered Neyland lore.

The stadium's East Upper Deck was just completed and Tartan Turf was new on the field when Bill Anderson and I began broadcasting Tennessee football over the Vol Network in 1968. The first home game was against Georgia, a team we hadn't played in 31 years. Down eight points with time expiring, Vol quarterback Bubba Wyche hit Gary Kries for a touchdown and then passed to Kenny DeLong for a two-point conversion that earned us an unbelievable tie. Just as exciting for Bill and me was discovering we could work together in the booth. We really didn't know before the game how it would go, and I remember that the chemistry among us and the staff was good that afternoon. It was the start of a wonderful, 31-

play made it happen for them, I was going to keep doing it.

Fortunately, there were lots of occasions to use the phrase. Tennessee maintained its winning tradition, and the stadium continued to grow, from a horseshoe to the perfect, double-decked bowl of today. For a couple of hours on a Saturday, it contains a population equivalent to the fifth largest city in Tennessee — and far more animated and colorful than any. It's a sight to behold.

For Bill and me, none of Neyland's structural changes meant more than enlarging the press box in 1987. Our radio booth was placed on a new bottom level of the box just above the stands. Over the repeated objection of the architect, I insisted that the window to the booth remain open. Which it did. So close were we now to fans that

> ## "For a couple of hours on a Saturday, (Neyland) contains a population equivalent to the fifth largest city in Tennessee — and far more animated and colorful than any."

year broadcasting relationship.

Calling a game for the ear presents a challenge. If you watch the behavior of fans at Neyland during a Vol scoring play, as I have, you'll see them rise to their feet and cheer in their excitement and maybe slap the back of the person next to them when the play is over. During those few seconds, emotions flow. But how do you give the person sitting at home in Decherd, following the game on the radio, the same sense of exhilaration as the person watching it from Seat 8, Row 24 in the stands?

During our maiden year at Neyland, I hit on a method. Instead of saying: "He's at the ten, five, TOUCHDOWN," I began to say: "He's at the ten...five...four...three...two...one. Give him, six! TOUCHDOWN, TENNESSEE." The slow countdown, which came to me in the creative heat of a game, allowed the excitement to build for listeners so they could savor the moment. And if stretching the end of the

those sitting below us could actually reach up and touch us. Hearing and feeling them right in front of us, in our laps almost, helped us relate to the hundred-thousand others in the bowl and convey their emotion to those who were miles away.

I'm proud of the role the Vol Network played in making Neyland more than a Knoxville site. It became, in essence, a statewide stadium. Almost anywhere in Tennessee you could hear the broadcast: sitting in a barbershop, flipping burgers in your backyard, strolling a golf course, fishing for bass on a nearby lake. During those few hours we were connected; we were all family, and Neyland was home.

There were other major contributors to the stadium's success. Better roads made access to Neyland easier for travelers from distant cities. The marketing of "Big Orange Country" kept enthusiasm for Vol football at a pitch. The "Pride of the Southland Marching Band," under Dr. Julian's guidance and now Dr. Sousa's, brought an exceptional level of spirit and pageantry to a sporting event. By design and by luck, these factors came together, so that at some point Neyland Stadium became more than a place to sit and watch a game. It became a place for celebration, and people kept coming back. Those who first met at the stadium when they were newlyweds ended up years later in the stands swapping stories about their grandchildren.

To be part of this has been an honor. So has the chance to witness deeds of valor. I remember back-to-back games against Alabama and Florida in 1970. In the first, young Bill Battle faced his own coach, the legendary "Bear" Bryant, a compassionate man who, nonetheless, projected an air of invincibility. Yet, we went out and beat Alabama, 24-0, that day, the first time they'd been shutout in 104 games. In the next game, we faced Florida. Their coach, Doug Dickey, wasn't the most popular man in Tennessee at the time, having left the Vols the year before. We annihilated the Gators, 38-7. After the game, Dickey stood on the south end of the field, turned toward the crowd and raised his fist in a salute to Big Orange superiority that day. It was a magnanimous gesture that I'll never forget.

I remember the running of Condredge Holloway, so gifted an athlete that he actually did better when plays broke down and he had to improvise on the field. I remember watching Georgia's Herschel Walker for the first time at Neyland. When we broke for commercial, I turned to Bill, who had played with Paul Hornung and Jim Taylor as an All-Pro receiver at Green Bay, and said of Walker, "He's a little different, isn't he?" "He's a lot different," said Bill. To put an exclamation on the point, later in the game talented defensive back Bill Bates executed a picture-perfect, open-field tackle on Walker, who ran right through him.

The most moving personal experience for me at Neyland came at halftime of the 1998 Kentucky game, our final broadcast ever from the stadium. Bill and I had already been honored by Coach Fulmer, who invited us to join the players and coaches for the traditional "Vol Walk" to the stadium before the game. A huge crowd lined the street for the event, and I kidded Peyton Manning after-

ward that we outdrew the attendance for his last walk the year before. By itself, this would have been a terrific send-off, but there was more.

At halftime, as I stood outside the booth taking a break, someone yelled, "Come back in; they're doing a show for you." Surely not, I thought. They would have told me. They hadn't. The band was playing my favorite tunes, and for the finale, country performer Kenny Chesney climbed a platform on the field and, accompanied by the band, sang a ballad he had written for my retirement. The presentation was a knockout.

I was standing in the booth, waving to Kenny and Gary Sousa in acknowledgment when suddenly I felt embarrassed. Then a wave of emotion hit me, and I was crying like a baby. I looked down in the stands and everyone I could see — thousands of people — were looking up at the booth, and many of them were crying, too. And as I looked around the stadium, I could see that while I'd been waving at Gary and Kenny, everyone was waving at us. I'll never forget that moment, for it captured the warm connection I've been privileged to have with Vols fans over so many years.

How did Neyland Stadium ever become what it is today? Did its growth flow from a grand design? I rather think it sprang from a kernel planted one afternoon in the late 1930s when General Neyland called one of his players, tackle Bob Woodruff, to his office. Like Neyland, Woodruff was an engineering student, and he admired and loved the General. Afraid he'd done something wrong, Woodruff instead heard the General say, simply: "Woodruff, you made an 'A' in chemistry. That's good, Woodruff."

That bit of interest and praise from a man customarily aloof from his players may have set something powerful in motion. Woodruff would become UT's athletic director, and the stadium would become to him more than a facility, more than a structure to hold people and play a game: it was the dream of a man he admired. With remarkable purpose and regularity, expansion project followed on expansion project under Woodruff and his chosen successor, Dickey. The fruition of the General's dream would be one of the most beautiful stadiums in America. Woodruff made an 'A.' The General made a remark. Maybe that's how it happened.

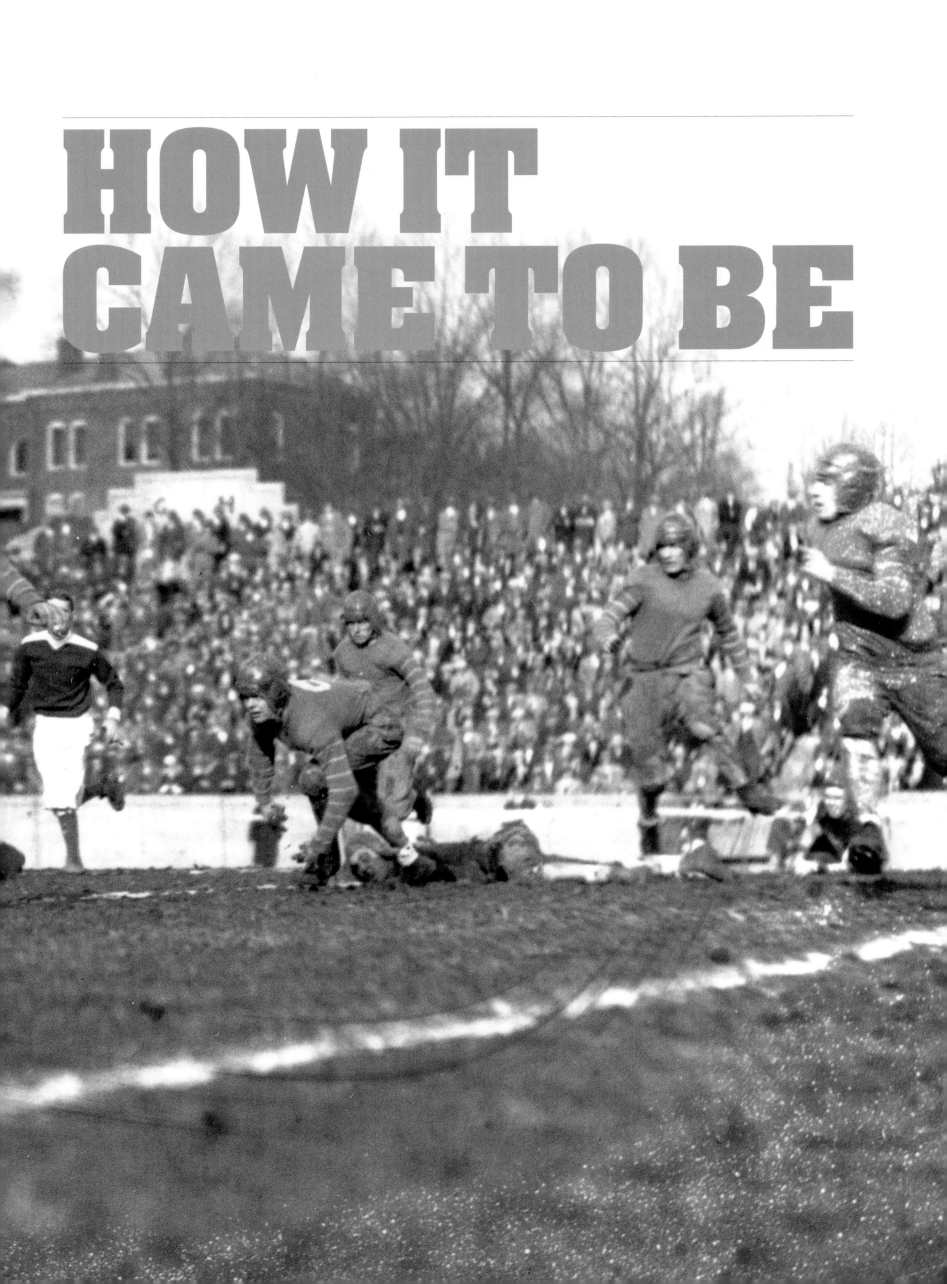

HOW IT CAME TO BE

For a moment, you be the visiting player. Two hours before kickoff, leave the cloister of your block-wall dressing room beneath the South Stands, turn left and left again and walk 30 yards through the dim-lit tunnel toward the field. As the opening grows larger, late morning light bursts through the gloom. One more step and you're there: the towering stadium rears into view and a space of majestic scale opens before you. Stop and turn in every direction. All about you, hundreds of rows of seats, topped by floors of glassed-in suites, climb to the sky. A still lake of perfectly groomed grass stretches before you. An ocean of silence greets you.

You slowly walk the grounds, absorbing the feel of the place. You won't, of course, know its legends or see its spirits. You won't find Billy Cannon stopped in mid-lunge at the north goal line, as 47,000 cheer, to preserve UT's 14-13 victory over the nation's top-ranked LSU Tigers in 1959. You won't see clearly embedded in the west stands the stadium's original 3,200 concrete seats, 2,000 of them empty for the field's first game played in a drizzle in 1921. You won't even know who Neyland is: UT's legendary, 21-season coach whom Oklahoma's Bud Wilkinson tabbed "the master of defense" and Knute Rockne called one of football's greatest.

But you will feel something. There have been too many remarkable plays on this hundred yards of ground, too many events of personal import, too many exalted moments, from victories savored to souls saved (at a Billy Graham Crusade), not to sense its history. And you will certainly know this: to play Tennessee in its hundred-thousand-seat shrine on a Saturday in fall is as big in the college sports world as it gets.

How did Tennessee football tradition sink such deep roots in this soil and how did the tiered temple called Neyland Stadium spring up around it? The story's beginning is humble enough, a tale of chert and mud. In 1891, 22 years after Princeton and Rutgers play the first collegiate football game, Tennessee fields a team for a one-game schedule, losing 24-0 to Sewanee in the mire in Chattanooga.

UT's first head coach won't arrive until 1899. Meanwhile, the rugby-like sport fights for a tenuous hold on campus. In 1892, UT wins its first game ever, 25-0, at neighboring Maryville College. The first home win comes the following year, also against outmanned Maryville, 32-0. After three seasons, however, the coachless Volunteers are only 4 and 10 against all opponents, and they field no intercollegiate team in 1894 and 1895. Notably, during this first foray into football, the school's orange and white colors are chosen. The selection is credited to Charles Moore, a member of the 1892 squad, who takes his inspiration from the orange center of the American daisy that spreads in profusion on the school's academic hill beside Cumberland Avenue.

Tennessee football fortunes take a positive turn with the birth of the Southern Intercollegiate Athletic Association in 1896. UT goes 4-0-0 that year followed by a 4-1-0 season in 1897. After a year off due to the Spanish-American War, the school opens the 1899 season under its first paid coach, J.A. Pierce. In two seasons, he crafts an 8-4-1 record and

introduces an era of itinerant coaches. Seven will come and go between 1899 and 1911, providing a mixed bag of results.

There are achievements in this period to cite. UT defeats Sewanee (in 1902) and Alabama (in 1904), both for the first time. The school's small, all-male band, a component of UT's military program, plays for the first time in support of the football program at the Sewanee game in 1902. Engineering professor R.C. "Red" Matthews brings

cheerleading and its megaphones to the sidelines in 1907. New player uniforms are selected: black jerseys with orange and white piping that runs the length of the sleeves. Nathan Washington Dougherty, a tall, raw-boned lineman called "Big-Un" by his Tennessee teammates, is an All-Southern selection in 1907 and 1908.

The team makes its home on Wait Field, located at the corner of 15th Street and Cumberland Avenue at the site of the present Walters Life Sciences Building. University historian Neal O'Steen writes of the hardship of playing at Wait where rock constantly works up from the hard-packed surface to scrape elbows and knees. Spectators

In rough-and-tumble early days of Vol football, there was little protection, except for cumbersome nose guards seen around the necks of several players in the pre-1900 team photo. And competition was uneven, from the University of Alabama to the Knoxville YMCA. Football, though, was gaining recognition on the bucolic, hilltop campus as the cover of the 1900 annual indicates. Shields-Watkins Field would later emerge between the academic buildings and the river. Previous spread: A Vol is pursued on muddy Shields-Watkins in the 1920s.

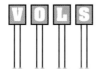

watch games from wooden benches or seat themselves on a high bank that bounds one side of the field.

Zora Clevenger, a former Indiana player, assumes UT coaching duties in 1911 and over five years fashions a commendable 26-15-2 record. Running a straight T formation, his 1914 team gives the school its first major success, compiling a 9-0-0 record en route to the SIAA championship. UT sweeps conference foes Alabama, 17-6; Kentucky, 7-0; Clemson, 27-0; Sewanee, 14-7; and Vanderbilt, its arch interstate rival, 16-14, in Nashville — UT's first ever football victory against Vandy. Nonconference foes take a shellacking as the Volunteers for the season score 374 points and yield 37. (Army, too, has an undefeated football season in 1914, and its star end, a gifted athlete from Texas named Robert Reese Neyland, will figure prominently in the evolution of UT's program.)

Even before UT's 1914 championship season, efforts are underway to find the team a new field. Football, baseball and track are all gaining in popularity, but Wait Field is hemmed by streets with no place to grow. As early as 1912, a seven-acre tract in a ravine that runs south of UT's hilltop campus

toward the Tennessee River is optioned by University Realty Company for a multipurpose athletic field. But efforts to pay the purchase price are halting, and soon the First World War intervenes, curtailing fundraising for the project and canceling the 1917 and 1918 football seasons.

Still owing $22,453 on the parcel in 1919 and having difficulty making

interest payments on the debt, the Realty Company finds a savior in Col. W.S. Shields, president of Knoxville's City National Bank. Shields agrees to pay the balance owed on the property if UT will prepare and equip an athletic field. His generous offer is accepted, and in November 1919, University trustees vote to name the field in honor of Shields and his wife, the former Alice Watkins: Shields-Watkins Field.

Shields later donates two more lots to the parcel. Dirt is moved from them and from the construction site of UT's Ayres Hall to fill a portion of the ravine. A 17-row, 3,200-seat grandstand is erected in late

Shown with the 1899 team and in the inset photo, J.A. Pierce was Tennessee's first paid coach. He left after two seasons with an 8-4-1 record. Until 1921, the Vols practiced and played on Wait Field on Cumberland Avenue. Its grassless, gravel-pitted surface added to the rugged character of the game. A 1909 program cover by renowned Knoxville artist Catherine Wiley is shown above. Below is the 1903 team.

"None were killed!

In addition to the injuries sustained by Miller and Peters, Spence was bruised about the face and French had a tooth disturbed."

Newspaper account of UT's 12-4 victory over Knoxville YMCA, 1894

1920 on the west side of the fill facing east. Fifteen-thousand cubic feet of steel-reinforced concrete are poured for the stands, which come none too soon. That October,

while UT is losing to Vanderbilt on Wait Field before a sizable crowd of 4,000, a rickety bleacher where the band is sitting collapses, spilling members and instruments down the side of a hill. Fortunately, no one is hurt, and the band plays on from chairs along the sideline.

In early 1921, the new grandstand, located a mile from Wait Field, faces a forlorn sight: an unmarked, ungraded expanse of mounds and gullies that turns a quagmire in the rain. University muscle power will be needed to fashion Shields-Watkins into a combined football field and baseball diamond with a quarter-mile track around it. March 16th is designated "Campus Day" as all classes are canceled and a volunteer work force of students and professors reports with wheelbarrows, picks and shovels. Working all day, they

help lay drainage pipes beneath the field, grade it and prepare a 20-foot-wide cinder-bed track. Women sweep the stands where they spread a lunch of sandwiches, cookies, fruit, hot coffee, cold buttermilk and ice cream cones for dessert. The task is completed by noon the next day.

The first game at Shields-Watkins Field is not football but baseball, played two days later, on March 19th, against Cincinnati University. Shields, the field's benefactor, throws the inaugural pitch to UT President H.A. Morgan, who whiffs so hard at the ball that he loses his balance and falls to the ground amid good-natured laughter. The first football game occurs six months later, on

Originally a division of UT's military department, the school's small, all-male band began to play at football games in 1902. The band had grown to 80 members by the 1930s, but majorettes didn't appear until a decade later. R.C. "Red" Matthews, an instructor in the school's engineering department, brought cheerleading to Vol games in 1907. The "Root-Leader," as he was called, used a megaphone and gymnastic moves to arouse crowd support.

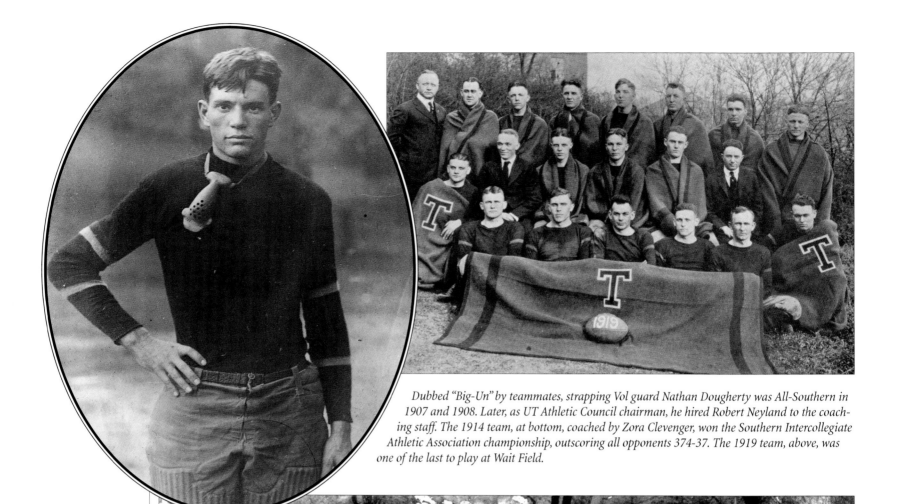

Dubbed "Big-Un" by teammates, strapping Vol guard Nathan Dougherty was All-Southern in 1907 and 1908. Later, as UT Athletic Council chairman, he hired Robert Neyland to the coaching staff. The 1914 team, at bottom, coached by Zora Clevenger, won the Southern Intercollegiate Athletic Association championship, outscoring all opponents 374-37. The 1919 team, above, was one of the last to play at Wait Field.

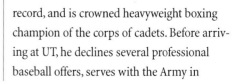

September 24, 1921. In a drizzling rain, with only 1,200 in the hard, wet concrete stands, UT defeats little Emory & Henry College, 27-0. Rufe Clayton scores the first Shields-Watkins touchdown on an 11-yard run. Volunteers hold opponents scoreless in all four games played at the new field that season — a splendid start to its stat sheet.

The 1921 season marks the coaching debut of M.B. Banks, who follows John Bender's fine three-year stint. Using a winged-T offense, Banks' five teams compile a 27-15-3 record. In 1921, UT joins the Southern Conference. A switch to orange jerseys comes the same year. In 1925, the

Beer Barrel is introduced as the coveted prize to the winner of the annual UT-Kentucky game, a practice that lasts until the 1999 season.

No event so influences UT's football program and stadium as the arrival in 1925 of a 34-year-old Army captain and football assistant, who divides his time this first year between working in the school's ROTC program and coaching ends for Banks. He's West Point Class of 1916 graduate Robert Neyland. His athletic exploits at the Academy are the subject of a Ripley "Believe It Or Not" cartoon: he stars on its nationally powerful football team, compiles a 35-5 pitching record, and is crowned heavyweight boxing champion of the corps of cadets. Before arriving at UT, he declines several professional baseball offers, serves with the Army in

France, studies graduate engineering at MIT and works as an aide to West Point Superintendent General Douglas MacArthur.

When Banks resigns in December 1925 to take a Knoxville high school coaching position, Nathan Dougherty, the former UT football standout, now a civil engineering dean and chairman of the school's Athletic Council, taps Neyland (pronounced KNEE-land) as Banks' successor. So begins the first of Neyland's three coaching eras (divided because of military service) that will encompass 21 seasons, from 1926 through 1952, and produce a .829 winning percentage (173-31-12), unequaled to this day by any person coaching NCAA football for 20 years or more. Serving both as UT's football coach and athletic director, Neyland will elevate the school's program to national prominence, shape the men who play for him,

As the 1920s approached, football games were drawing as many as 4,000 spectators to Wait Field, particularly against arch rivals such as Vanderbilt. Above, the 1919 Vol team stands on the sidelines, and at bottom, students form a conga line. A section of the wooden stands collapsed in 1920, spilling band members on the field, but injury was averted and the band played on.

expand the stadium through major additions, and enshrine himself in college football's Hall of Fame.

Neyland brings Tennessee an efficient single-wing offense and an opportunistic defense that cut a swath through the conference. Assisted by two former West Point teammates, Paul Parker and W.H. (Bill) Britton, he coaches with the strategy and preparation of a commander sending troops into battle. His teams are known for their ability to execute with precision, maintain excellent field position, apply constant pressure that forces opponents' mistakes, and remain mentally tough in adversity. "We won because we knew we were better prepared than the other team," halfback Buddy Hackman will say later of Neyland, who

needed to do little coaching once a game began. "Neyland gave us the edge."

As lopsided as the modern UT-

Vanderbilt series is, it's startling to recall how completely Vanderbilt dominated the early years of the rivalry. When Neyland begins his first year as head coach and athletic director in 1926, UT's record against Vanderbilt, then a football powerhouse, is a dismal 2-17-2. Equally galling is Vanderbilt's insistence that the popular series be played only at its commodious, 20,000-seat Dudley Field, disdaining little Shields-Watkins, whose flat surface proves inefficient for drainage. "Now that Tennessee's football season is practically over, athletic authorities should begin to make a football field of Shields-Watkins," observes UT's student newspaper in derisive tones in 1925. "Fans are tired of seeing Tennessee's wonderful football team play in a sea of mud."

While banking on Neyland to "even the score with Vanderbilt" (Neyland obliges, with a 16-3-2 record in his coaching tenure), Dougherty addresses the field's inadequacies. Before the 1926 season begins, he has the playing surface sodded after it's worked into a sloping,

turtle-back shape that promotes water run-off into catch basins. In response to growing season ticket sales and the draw of the Vanderbilt game, he adds the 17-row East Stands with 3,600 pine-board seats and team locker rooms beneath, erects wooden bleachers at the south end zone for overflow crowds, and marks off a practice field beyond the bleachers so Shields-Watkins can stay in good shape for games.

Neyland gives Dougherty everything he hopes for in 1926, except a win over Vanderbilt, which will come two years later. Allyn McKeen scores the first UT touchdown of the Neyland era, picking up his own fumble and scoring from 11 yards out. The Volunteers finish the season 8-1-0, undefeated at home and losing only to Vanderbilt in Nashville. In 1927, the surging Vols tie Vanderbilt and

beat everyone else, winning the Southern Conference Championship with an 8-0-1 record. UT's freshman team is also undefeated, outscoring opponents 160-14.

Thus begins a remarkable period of winning consistency. From 1926 through 1932, Neyland's teams lose only twice. From the beginning of the 1925 season, when Neyland is an assistant, to the third game of the 1933 season, Tennessee is unbeaten at Shields-Watkins, amassing 55 victories and three ties. Neyland's overall record from 1926 through 1934, when he leaves for a year to command a battalion of Army combat engineers in the Panama Canal Zone, is an astounding 76-7-5, including undefeated streaks of 33 and 28 games.

UT's program attains national prominence in October 1928 with the defeat of Alabama at Tuscaloosa, where the powerful Crimson Tide, winner of the two previous Rose Bowls, is prohibitively favored. Sophomore Gene McEver, who teams with fellow halfback Buddy Hackman to form the Vols' vaunted "Hack and Mack" attack that year, returns the game's opening kickoff 98 yards for a touchdown. Joined in the backfield by ball-handling wizard, quarterback Bobby Dodd, the duo leads a young Tennessee team to a 15-13 victory and places the Vols for the first time among college football's elite.

As the "Flaming Sophomores" of the 1928 team mature, Tennessee dominates its schedules, posting records of 9-0-1 in 1929, 9-1-0 in 1930, 9-0-1 in 1931 and 9-0-1 in 1932. By comparison, 1933 (7-3-0) and 1934 (8-2-0) are mediocre years for the Vols. Tennessee begins placing men

John Bender, who played at Nebraska, coached the Vols from 1916 through 1920, compiling an 18-5-4 record. He's at bottom right with assistant coaches Hobt, left, and Kriger. Willis McCabe, above, was Tennessee's All-Southern quarterback in 1919. Wait Field opponents ranged from Tusculum and Carson-Newman to South Carolina and Kentucky.

After 50,000 yards of fill dirt was hauled to the site in a ravine and the concrete, 3,200-seat West Stands was poured, 2,000 UT students and faculty donated two days of work in March 1921 to help prepare Shields-Watkins Field, breaking for lunch in the stands. The first football game was played September 24, 1921, the Vols defeating Emory & Henry, 27-0. Following spread: Resembling a scrum is the collision of Vols and a white jerseyed opponent at Shields-Watkins.

on the 11-member consensus All-America team. McEver is the first, selected in 1929 after leading the nation in scoring with 130 points. He's followed by Dodd in 1930, guard Herman Hickman in 1931 and halfback Beattie Feathers in 1933. When New York City's mayor wants to sponsor a charity game in 1930 to offset the growing gloom of the Depression, he asks the heralded Vols to play New York University at Yankee Stadium. Tennessee wins 13-0.

Vol success translates into more seats at home. In May 1929, trustees approve a 42-row, 11,060-seat addition to the West Stands, bringing Shields-Watkins' capacity to 17,860. That's not enough for the season's

Alabama game that draws 23,000 spectators. They overflow the stands and bleachers and cover the end zones and the slope north of the field. Impressed by Tennessee's football success, Dougherty and the trustees pledge to add seating "as fast as attendance at Vol football games necessitates."

Tennessee joins the fledgling Southeastern Conference in 1933 as the nation sinks deeper into the Depression. The price of a season ticket to Shields-Watkins is reduced from ten to seven dollars; single tickets go for fifty cents. Average attendance for the year climbs above 10,000 for six games, though high-profile match-ups strain the field's capacity. A public address system is installed to relate play results to the crowd.

Volunteer end coach and scout, Bill Britton, serves as interim head

coach in 1935 while Neyland is in Panama. When he returns as a newly retired Army major, he begins rebuilding a program that posted a 4-5-0 record in his absence. The record improves to 6-2-2 in 1936 and 6-3-1 in 1937, before a three-year campaign begins that results in 30 consecutive regular season victories, three SEC championships, Orange, Sugar and Rose bowl appearances, and two national championships as proclaimed by Litkenhous and Dunkel football rating services in 1938 and Litkenhous and Williamson in 1940.

On the eve of this amazing run, trustees

enlarge the field. In 1937, they approve a 1,500-seat addition adjacent to the West Stands. Known as Section X, it contains within it an armory and basement-level rifle range for the school's ROTC program, making the project eligible for federal construction funds and WPA labor. Though the field now accommodates 19,360 fans, it draws overflow crowds of 25,000 for both the Alabama game, broadcast to a national radio audience that October, and the Vanderbilt

Rangy Estes Kefauver, at right, of Madisonville, Tennessee, who played tackle for the Vols in 1922 and 1923, later served as a U.S. Senator and ran as the Democratic candidate for Vice President in 1956. Above, teammate Jimmie Smith played halfback and quarterback. Opposite page: Captain Robert Neyland, hat in hand, joined the coaching staff of M. Beal Banks in 1925 and became head coach the following year as Shields-Watkins' East Stands was added.

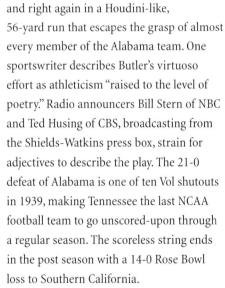

game in November.

Prior to the 1938 season, as a gifted group of sophomores prepares to join the varsity, a major expansion is under way. The East Stands are enlarged by 12,030 seats, bringing capacity to 31,390. A four-floor dormitory is built beneath the sloping stands to house 128 male students, half of them athletes. The band occupies a practice room in the building the next year.

The Vols exceed expectations for 1938, posting an 11-0-0 record that includes a win over Oklahoma in the January 1, 1939, Orange Bowl. Captained by end Bowden Wyatt, the team claims such Vol greats as backs George "Bad News" Cafego and Walter "Babe" Wood and linemen Abe Shires and Bob Suffridge. Their 14-6 victory over LSU in October is watched by 36,000 at Shields-Watkins, the largest crowd at the time ever to witness a sporting event in Tennessee.

Perhaps the most remarkable touchdown run in the field's history occurs in 1939 against Alabama. Johnny Butler, a 160-pound Vol sophomore halfback, takes a hand-off and cuts right, then left across field and right again in a Houdini-like, 56-yard run that escapes the grasp of almost every member of the Alabama team. One sportswriter describes Butler's virtuoso effort as athleticism "raised to the level of poetry." Radio announcers Bill Stern of NBC and Ted Husing of CBS, broadcasting from the Shields-Watkins press box, strain for adjectives to describe the play. The 21-0 defeat of Alabama is one of ten Vol shutouts in 1939, making Tennessee the last NCAA football team to go unscored-upon through a regular season. The scoreless string ends in the post season with a 14-0 Rose Bowl loss to Southern California.

The 1940 team maintains the standard of the previous two years as it compiles a 10-0 regular season record. UT claims the NCAA record for holding regular season opponents scoreless for consecutive quarters — 71 — from the second quarter of the 1938 LSU game through the second quarter of the

"Making a field of Shields-Watkins will, if nothing more,
reduce the athletic department's
laundry bill."

1925 UT student newspaper critcizing the field of mud upon which the football team played.

Coach Neyland surrounded himself with former West Point teammates Paul Parker, left, and Bill Britton, who served as assistants. The line for his 1926 single-wing formation, above, included two future coaches: John Barnhill (Tennessee and Arkansas), third from right, and Allyn McKeen (Mississippi State), far right. In the backfield are Elmore, Dodson, quarterback Harkness and Rice.

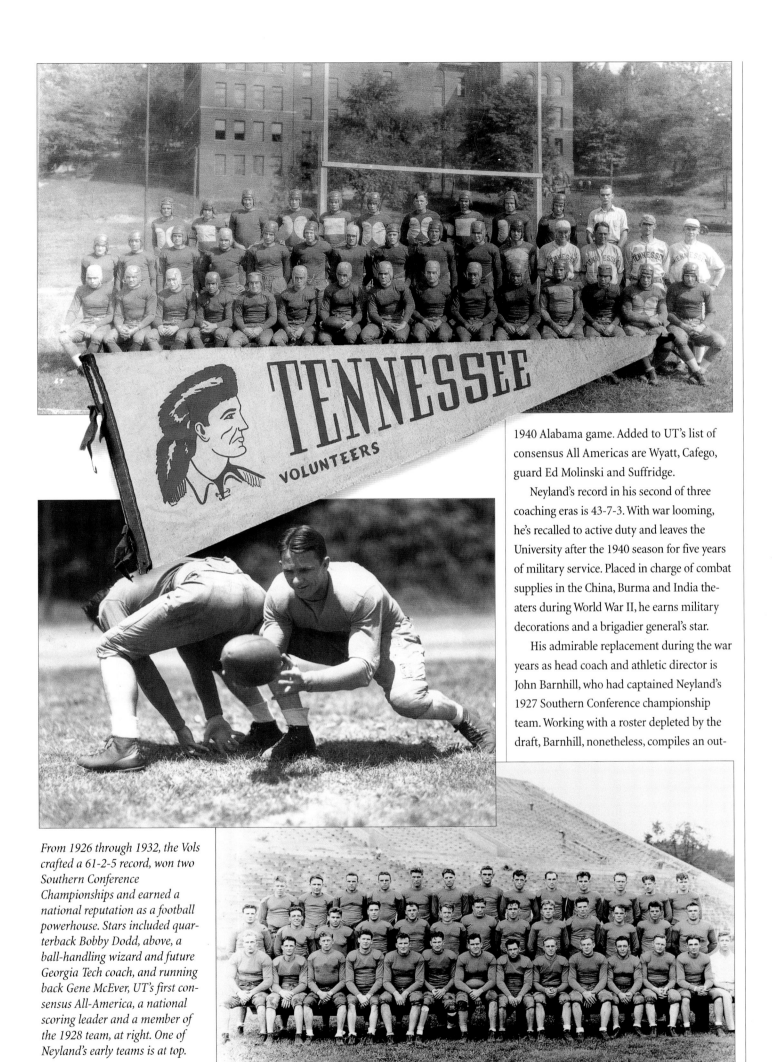

1940 Alabama game. Added to UT's list of consensus All Americas are Wyatt, Cafego, guard Ed Molinski and Suffridge.

Neyland's record in his second of three coaching eras is 43-7-3. With war looming, he's recalled to active duty and leaves the University after the 1940 season for five years of military service. Placed in charge of combat supplies in the China, Burma and India theaters during World War II, he earns military decorations and a brigadier general's star.

His admirable replacement during the war years as head coach and athletic director is John Barnhill, who had captained Neyland's 1927 Southern Conference championship team. Working with a roster depleted by the draft, Barnhill, nonetheless, compiles an out-

From 1926 through 1932, the Vols crafted a 61-2-5 record, won two Southern Conference Championships and earned a national reputation as a football powerhouse. Stars included quarterback Bobby Dodd, above, a ball-handling wizard and future Georgia Tech coach, and running back Gene McEver, UT's first consensus All-America, a national scoring leader and a member of the 1928 team, at right. One of Neyland's early teams is at top.

15

standing 32-5-2 record and takes Tennessee to the Sugar Bowl and Rose Bowl. When Neyland returns, Barnhill moves to Arkansas to become a successful head coach and athletics director at that school. The University remembers four players who die in active duty in the war — Clyde Fuson, Bill Nowling, Rudy Klarer and Willis Tucker — by retiring their jersey numbers: 32, 49, 61, 62.

Upon his return to UT, Neyland predicts it will "take us five years to put Tennessee back on top." He's prophetic,

Forty-two rows (11,000 seats) had been added to the West Stands at Shields-Watkins Field, bringing capacity to nearly 18,000, when the game, at bottom, was played in the early or mid 1930s. An artist rendering of the field on the opposite page is from the same era. Excitement about the Vol program was rising, as witness a homecoming motorcade in Knoxville and the charity game with NYU at Yankee Stadium in 1930. Following spread: Games with touted teams packed Shields-Watkins, where spectators lined the end zones and perched on the north slope.

THE SHIELDS-WATKINS STADIUM, KNOXVILLE, TENN.—76

though he may not have foreseen the roller coaster ride it would be. It begins well enough in 1946 when the Vols tie for first in the SEC with a 9-2-0 record. One of the toughest players to wear Tennessee pads, tackle Dick Huffman, is a consensus All-America. But back-to-back .500 seasons in 1947 (5-5-0) and 1948 (4-4-2) have some wondering aloud if the General has lost

continued on page 23

17

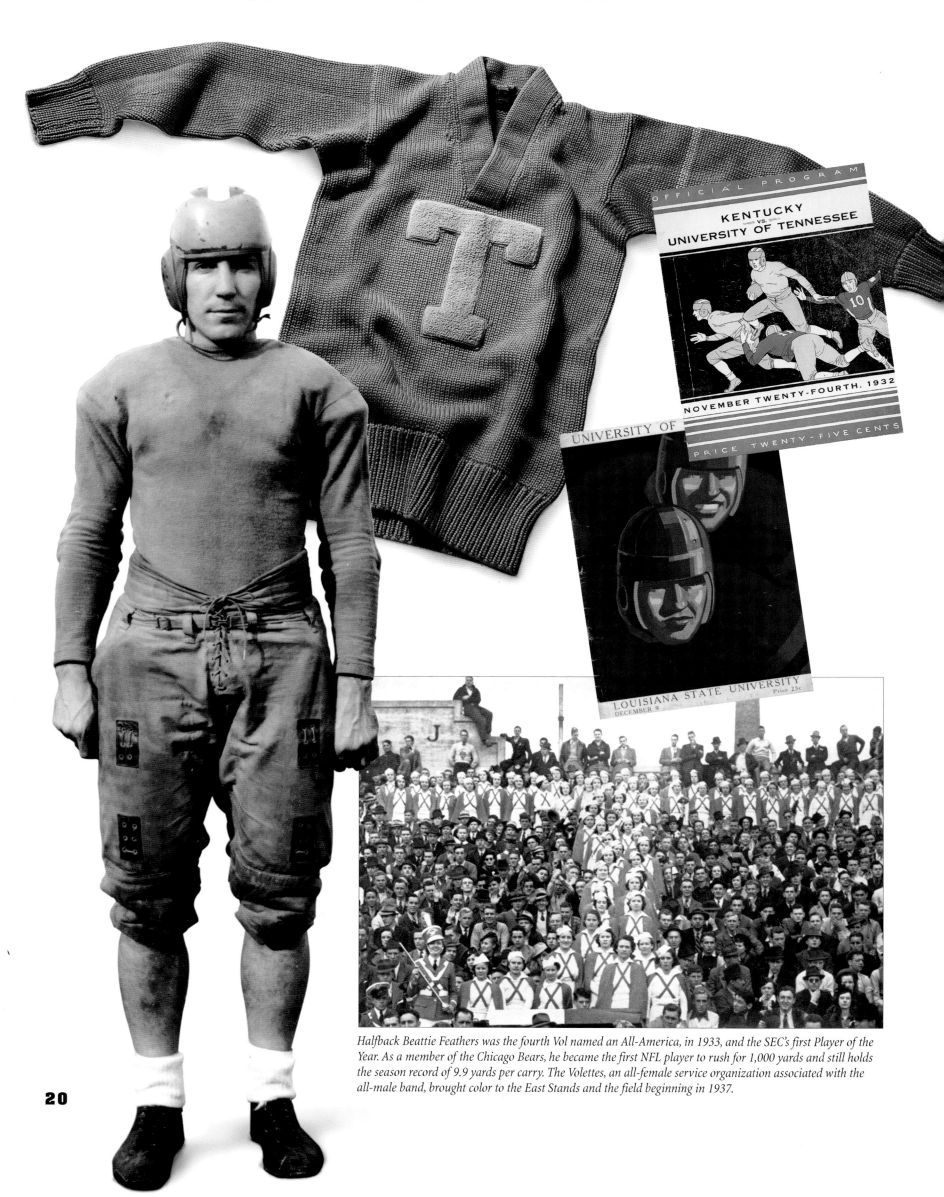

OFFICIAL PROGRAM

KENTUCKY
vs.
UNIVERSITY OF TENNESSEE

NOVEMBER TWENTY-FOURTH, 1932

PRICE TWENTY-FIVE CENTS

UNIVERSITY OF

LOUISIANA STATE UNIVERSITY   Price 25c
DECEMBER 9

Halfback Beattie Feathers was the fourth Vol named an All-America, in 1933, and the SEC's first Player of the Year. As a member of the Chicago Bears, he became the first NFL player to rush for 1,000 yards and still holds the season record of 9.9 yards per carry. The Volettes, an all-female service organization associated with the all-male band, brought color to the East Stands and the field beginning in 1937.

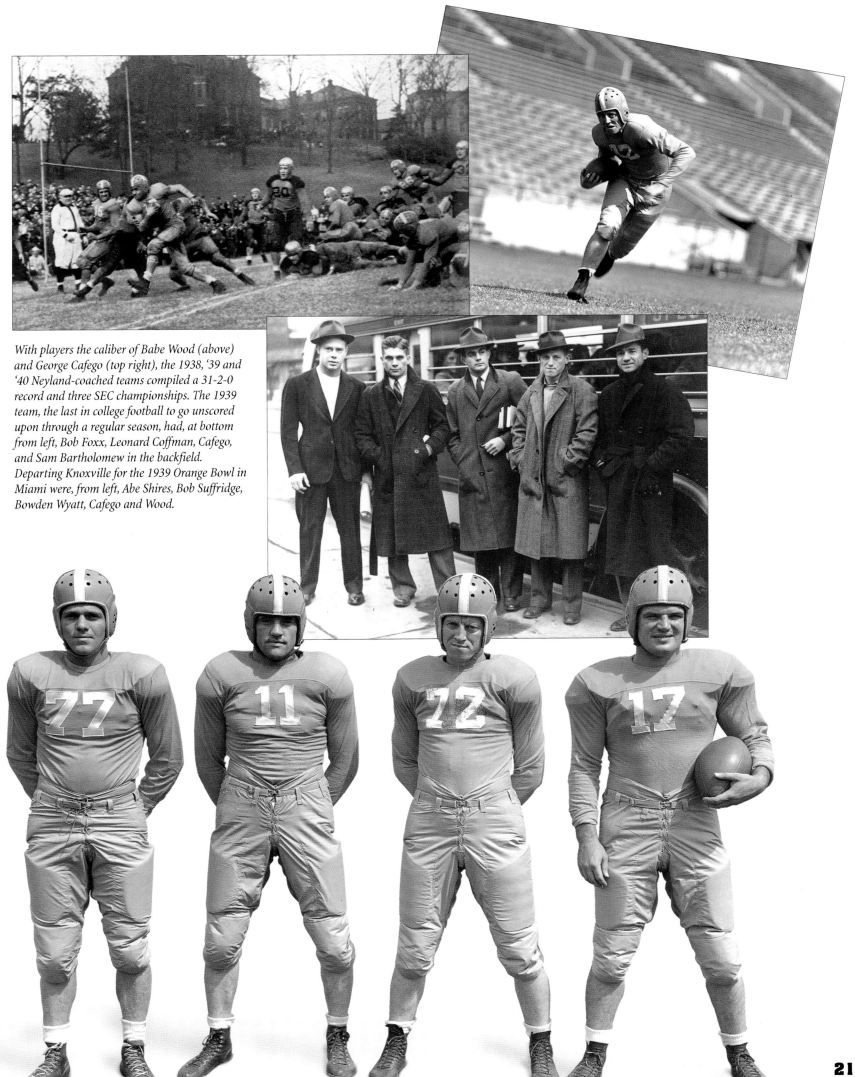

With players the caliber of Babe Wood (above) and George Cafego (top right), the 1938, '39 and '40 Neyland-coached teams compiled a 31-2-0 record and three SEC championships. The 1939 team, the last in college football to go unscored upon through a regular season, had, at bottom from left, Bob Foxx, Leonard Coffman, Cafego, and Sam Bartholomew in the backfield. Departing Knoxville for the 1939 Orange Bowl in Miami were, from left, Abe Shires, Bob Suffridge, Bowden Wyatt, Cafego and Wood.

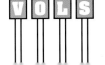

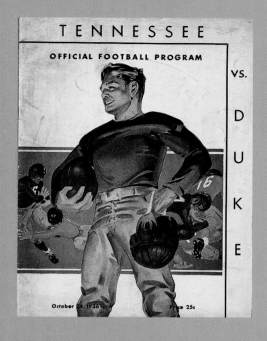

TENNESSEE
OFFICIAL FOOTBALL PROGRAM
VS. DUKE
October 26, 1935   Price 25c

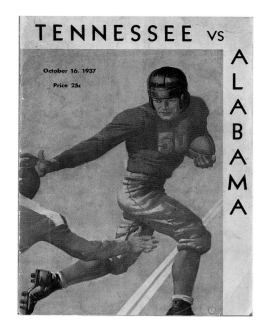

TENNESSEE vs ALABAMA
October 16, 1937
Price 25c

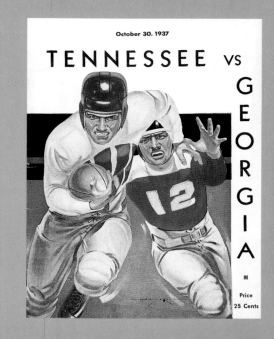

October 30, 1937
TENNESSEE vs GEORGIA
Price 25 Cents

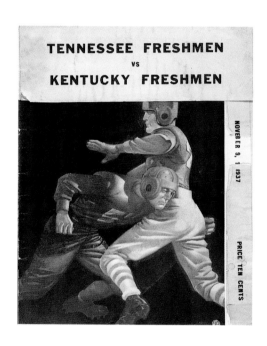

TENNESSEE FRESHMEN
vs
KENTUCKY FRESHMEN
NOVEMBER 9, 1937
PRICE TEN CENTS

TENNESSEE vs VANDERBILT
Nov. 13, 1937   Price 25c

THE TENNESSEE GRIDIRON
TENNESSEE vs L.S.U.
OCTOBER 29, 1938   PRICE 25c

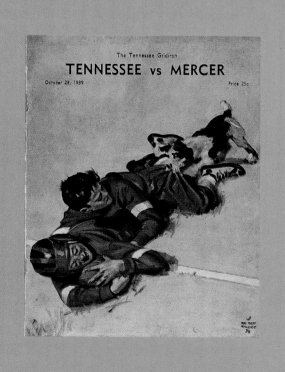

The Tennessee Gridiron
TENNESSEE vs MERCER
October 28, 1939   Price 25c

The Tennessee Gridiron
TENNESSEE vs KENTUCKY
November 23, 1940   Price 25c

Tennessee vs Fordham
October 1942   Price 25c

his touch. He understands their reaction. "I don't care what endeavor you go into," he tells a player who is disturbed by the rare criticism aimed at Neyland, "you can't live on your clippings. You must produce."

Betting Neyland and his team will do that, the school undertakes in 1948 the largest Shields-Watkins expansion project to that time. It constructs the $1.5 million curved South Stands which adds 15,000 seats, creating a long-sought, horseshoe-shaped stadium with a capacity of 46,390. The project also helps relieve a campus housing shortage created by the enrollment of World War II veterans returning to school on the GI Bill. Stadium Hall is built beneath the stands with 166 dorm rooms as well as space for the athletic department and a dressing room for vis-

iting teams. A record 48,000 watch UT defeat Alabama that season. Two weeks later, 52,000 crowd the stadium to see Tennessee almost tie top-ranked North Carolina.

The school's faith in the football program is rewarded. The team is 7-2-1 in 1949 and third in the SEC. Once again Neyland has a talented group of sophomores to lead the effort into 1950. That team, considered one of his best, goes 11-1-0, upsetting Texas in the Cotton Bowl on New Year's Day. Dunkel proclaims the team the national champion, and the bowl victory stakes Tennessee to a preseason claim to No. 1 the following fall.

Behind tailback Hank Lauricella, a consensus All-America and Heisman Trophy runner-up, and tackle Doug Atkins, who is later named SEC "Player of the Quarter Century," the Vols go undefeated in 1951 and are named national

"*My* field will be ready! What about *your* team?"

Groundskeeper Deanie Hoskins' traditional response to Coach Neyland's annual question: "Will the field be ready by September?"

Opponents faced the hard-nosed, 1940 Vol line of, at bottom from left, Jimmy Coleman, Abe Shires, Ed Molinski, Norbert Ackerman, Bob Suffridge, Bill Luttrell and Ed Cifers. Ackerman, the Vol captain, led the team onto the field against Duke in 1940. Groundskeeper Deanie Hoskins, at top, tended Shields-Watkins' turf from 1926 until 1961.

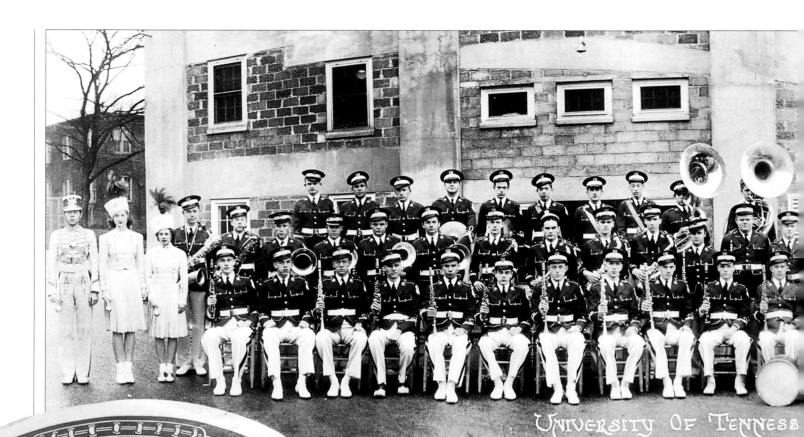

UNIVERSITY OF TENNESS

champions by Associated Press and United Press as well as Williamson and Litkenhous, making it a consensus choice. The title is based on regular season performance — a good thing since Tennessee loses to Maryland in the Sugar Bowl. As Neyland predicted, Tennessee sits atop the college football world.

Neyland's ability to exploit opponents' mistakes and command superior effort from his players is still discussed today. Dr. Andy Kozar, a fullback on the 1950 and 1951 teams and the hero of the Cotton Bowl victory over Texas, recalls the coach's no-nonsense ways. "He told it

As a division of the University's military department, the 1940 band had male musicians only, though coeds filled the ranks during the war years. Majorettes arrived in the 1940s, and the growing band became known as the "Pride of the Southland" in 1950. Major Walter Ryba, who succeeded Ernest Hall as director, raised the level of halftime entertainment, and Dr. W.J. Julian (1961 to 1993) took his now non-military, coed band to national prominence. Cheerleading squads rallied support from the student section at the south end of the East Stands.

K-43—Shields-Watkins Stadium,
University of Tennessee, Knoxville, Tenn

In 1938, above, 10,030 seats were added to the East Stands, bringing capacity to 31,390. Below the 44 new rows were dorm rooms, half of them for players. Ten years later, in the largest expansion project at Shields-Watkins Field to that time, the firm that built the replica of the Parthenon in Nashville constructed the South Stands in 1948, adding 15,000 seats resulting in a horseshoe-shaped stadium that accommodated 46,390. Stadium Hall, a dormitory built into the stands, relieved a campus housing shortage from enrollment of World War II veterans on the GI Bill. Ironically, General Neyland was suffering his worst seasons at the time, but the school's faith in his ultimate success was rewarded. Tennessee climbed from 4-4-2 in 1948 to the pinnacle of the college football world as national champions three years later. The frame of Knoxville's Baptist Hospital rises across the river.

like it was, and he was eminently fair," says Kozar. "He was unimpressed with credentials; he wanted performance. Those who practiced the best played for him."

Back in 1949, Kozar wonders if he'll have that chance. Recruited by a number of universities, the Pennsylvania high school athlete chooses UT where the people he meets are "so receptive, genuine and wonderful" to the son of a coal-mining family. But two weeks after arriving on campus, he breaks his collarbone in a scrimmage. A Pittsburgh University recruiter tracks down the dejected player, warns him he will be dropped from the team and urges him to accept a Pittsbureh scholarship and leave. "When Neyland heard about this, he came to the hospital to see me," says Kozar of the coach known for his aloofness. "'I don't know whether you'll play football or not at Tennessee,' he told me, 'but you will keep your scholarship.'" Kozar is relieved, knowing the pledge will be honored.

While Tennessee is producing two of its finest football seasons, average attendance at the 46,390-seat stadium is at half capacity: 24,910 in 1950 and 23,961 in 1951. One reason is a home schedule that includes "breathers" against the caliber of the University of Chattanooga, Tennessee Tech and Washington and Lee. In pre-interstate-travel days when a trip from Nashville to Knoxville is a hard, five-hour drive and one from Memphis to East Tennessee seems as arduous as a cross-country journey, fans show up in large numbers only for games against nationally powerful rivals like Alabama and LSU.

At the half-century mark, Shields-Watkins Field is growing not only in size but tradition. The band, dubbed "Pride of the Southland" by *Knoxville Journal* sports writer Ed Harris in 1950, has become an integral part of game-day festivities. The small, all-male military band that first roots the Vols to a 6-0 victory over Sewanee in 1902 has grown into a marching musical ensemble that includes female majorettes. Though still under the jurisdiction of the school's military department, the Pride of the Southland Marching Band, under the direction of Major Walter Ryba, who once played in John Philip Sousa's band, shows a theatrical bent as it performs theme-oriented halftime shows that include minstrels and hillbilly reviews.

The band's rise to the nation's elite will occur when it is transferred from the military to the music education department and Dr. W. J. Julian begins a three-decade tenure as director in 1961. He brings new uniforms

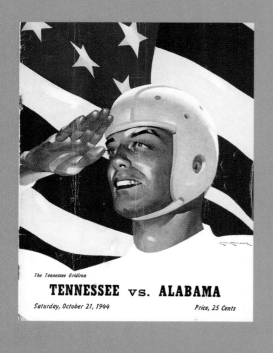

The Tennessee Gridiron

TENNESSEE vs. ALABAMA

Saturday, October 21, 1944   Price, 25 Cents

THE TENNESSEE GRIDIRON

U.S. NAVY

TENNESSEE
VS.
NORTH CAROLINA
SHIELDS-WATKINS FIELD
SATURDAY, NOVEMBER 2, 1945

OFFICIAL 25¢ PROGRAM

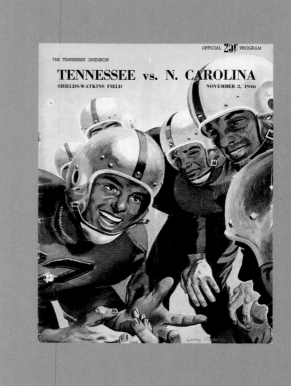

OFFICIAL 25¢ PROGRAM

THE TENNESSEE GRIDIRON

TENNESSEE vs. N. CAROLINA

SHIELDS-WATKINS FIELD   NOVEMBER 2, 1946

GA. TECH vs. TENNESSEE

SEPTEMBER 27, 1947   PRICE 35c

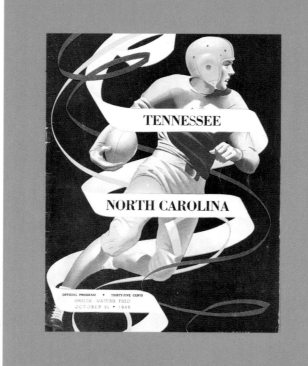

TENNESSEE
NORTH CAROLINA

OFFICIAL PROGRAM • THIRTY-FIVE CENTS
SHIELDS-WATKINS FIELD
OCTOBER 30 • 1948

OFFICIAL PROGRAM • THIRTY-FIVE CENTS

TENNESSEE vs ALABAMA

SHIELDS-WATKINS FIELD • OCTOBER 16 • 1948

OFFICIAL PROGRAM • THIRTY-FIVE CENTS

TENNESSEE
GA. TECH

SHIELDS-WATKINS FIELD NEWS, SEPTEMBER 23, 1950

TENNESSEE
MISS. SOUTHERN

ALSO BOASTS
ENSIVE POWERS

23

COACHES SATISFIED
TEAMS ARE READY

OFFICIAL PROGRAM • THIRTY-FIVE CENTS

OFFICIAL PROGRAM • THIRTY-FIVE CENTS

TENNESSEE
MISSISSIPPI

NOVEMBER 18 • 1950 • SHIELDS-WATKINS FIELD

The playing field fashioned by students and teachers from the ravine below UT's landmark Ayres Hall and above the Tennessee River in 1921 had evolved into an impressive stadium by mid century, and spirit on the growing state university campus was soaring as Vol football tradition and ritual took hold. The original 17 rows of seats are outlined at the bottom of the West Stands (the section holding the press box).

VOLS

"It has been said that there is guts at both ends of a bayonet. Well, there is guts, too, at both ends of a tackle."

Coach (and brigadier general) Robert Neyland

and innovative marching drills as the band grows in size and reputation. By 1964, it boasts 140 men and women, a number that more than doubles by the end of the century. In 1972, the band introduces a new fight song that fans at the stadium immediately embrace — "Rocky Top." The band's ritualistic pregame march from the music building to the stadium, its forming of the "T" at the emotion-charged start of a game and its

intricate halftime marching shows are beloved by Vol fans. These colorful traditions are carried forward by current director Dr. Gary Sousa (who claims no relationship to John Philip, but how perfect a name) and his staff.

At mid-century, mascots are finding their place on the sidelines at Shields-Watkins Field. A bluetick coonhound called Smokey makes his appearance in 1953. At a student-sponsored contest during

During World War II, Robert Neyland earned his brigadier general's star, but football wasn't far from mind, as a Pacific battlefield diagram shows. In Neyland's absence, John Barnhill compiled a 32-5-2 record, leading Tennessee to the Sugar and Rose bowls. When the General returned to UT, celebration was in order, as in his victory ride after a Kentucky game.
Following spread: All-America back Hank Lauricella, seated beside Neyland, helped the Vols attain the national championship in 1951.

halftime of the Mississippi State game that season, a number of native-bred Tennessee "houn' dogs" audition for the crowd. As each is introduced, the student body cheers for its favorite. When it comes the turn of "Blue Smokey," owned by the Rev. W.C. Brooks, the dog barks at hearing the sound of his name over the loudspeaker. The crowd roars and the dog barks again, creating an instant bond. There have been eight Smokeys over the years, all raised by the same Knoxville family and descended from the original hound, who made his mascot debut at the 1953 Kentucky game. Beside baying at opposing players and mascots, Smokey, with big ears flapping, leads the team through the giant "T" prior to the start of every home game.

Other traditions take root. Beginning

with the 1965 season, a Tennessee Walking Horse, another native breed, begins cantering around the field before each game as the crowd roars. The horse disappears when artificial turf is placed on the field, making turns difficult for the high-stepping animal, but reappears when a grass surface is restored. The Volunteer, a student dressed in buckskin and a coonskin hat, emerges to lead cheers while carrying a huge orange Vol flag. For years, the student section holds up multicolored cards on cue to spell out messages and create designs during a game.

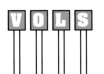

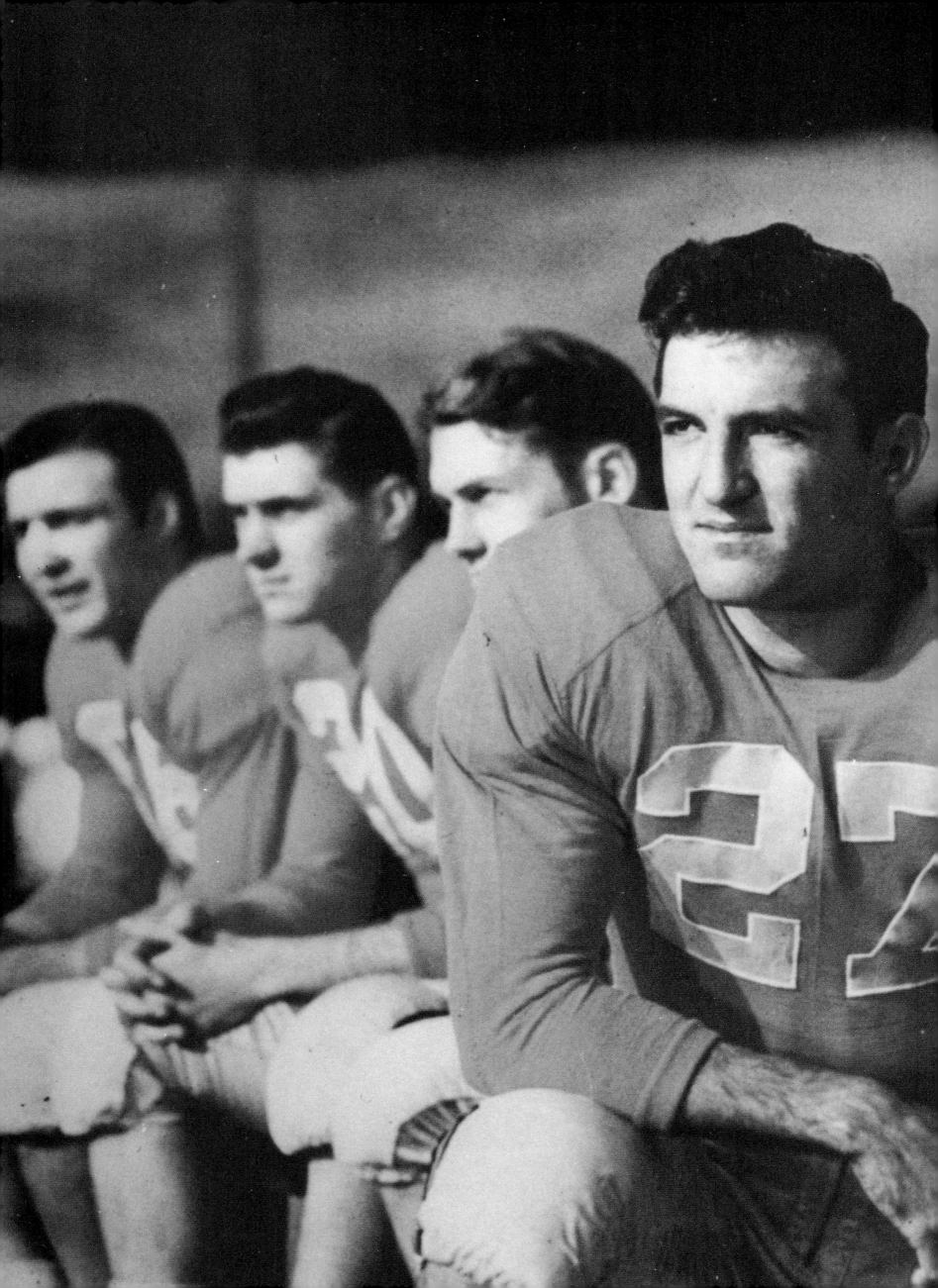

The program grows old enough to create its own legends. One is Mickey O'Brien, UT's Hall of Fame trainer, who becomes an integral part of the football staff, which he serves from 1938 to 1972. Another is John Deanie Hoskins, who begins tending the turf on Shields-Watkins in 1921, its first season, and cares for it like a doting parent for more than 30 years. In what becomes

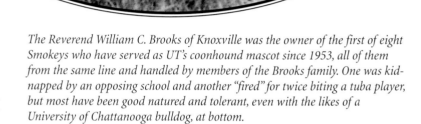

The Reverend William C. Brooks of Knoxville was the owner of the first of eight Smokeys who have served as UT's coonhound mascot since 1953, all of them from the same line and handled by members of the Brooks family. One was kidnapped by an opposing school and another "fired" for twice biting a tuba player, but most have been good natured and tolerant, even with the likes of a University of Chattanooga bulldog, at bottom.

and guard John Michels, goes 8-1-1. The health of the legendary coach is beginning to fail, and he relinquishes the strain of coaching to serve solely as UT's athletic director. During his last coaching era, he is 54-17-4. His overall record at UT includes nine undefeated seasons, five conference titles, and

three teams heralded as national champions, one by consensus. No one in the college ranks has ever coached so long (21 years) while maintaining so high a winning percentage as Neyland. In a fitting finale to an epic tenure, he directs the Vols to a 46-0 rout of Vanderbilt in his last game. With that victory, Neyland, who was hired in part to settle the score with Vanderbilt, brings the series that once heavily favored the Commodores to a 21-21-4 mark.

Harvey Robinson, who played tailback

a traditional exchange before each season, Neyland asks the proud groundskeeper if the field will be ready in September. "My field will be ready," Hoskins always retorts. "What about your team?" Spectators establish their own rituals, buying season tickets for seats that are handed down from one generation to the next, nurturing lifelong friendships in the stands, so that a trip to Shields-Watkins is like a block party — a boisterous neighborhood get-together.

Neyland finishes his illustrious coaching career at the end of the 1952 regular season after his team, led by captain Jim Haslam and two All-Americas, tackle Doug Atkins

Bowden Wyatt, an All-America end who was captain of Neyland's undefeated 1938 team, assumed the UT coaching mantle in 1955. His 1956 team posted a 10-0 regular-season record and claimed the SEC crown. Wyatt, who spent eight years at the helm of the Volunteers, was one of 20 former Neyland players to enter the college coaching ranks. He was inducted in the College Football Hall of Fame as a player and a coach, having won championships at Arkansas and Wyoming as well.

for Neyland in the early 1930s and was a talented backfield coach on his staff, is elevated to head coach upon Neyland's retirement. In 1953 and 1954, he compiles a combined 10-10-1 record. Neyland dismisses Robinson after the 1954 season, calling the action "the hardest thing I've ever had to do." Robinson leaves for Florida, later to return to UT as an assistant, and Neyland installs another protege, Bowden Wyatt, as head coach for the 1955 season. The handsome, 38-year-old Wyatt, who helped lead UT to an 11-0 record in 1938 as an All-America end, returns to his alma mater after head coaching stints at Wyoming and Arkansas.

What follows are three fat years and seven lean ones. They span Wyatt's tenure from 1955 through 1962 as well as Jim McDonald's .500 coaching season in 1963 and the first year, 1964, for Doug Dickey, who will return Tennessee football to prominence. During the years in decline, UT records three losing seasons and never manages more than six victories in any season, a lackluster performance for a team that's been to the top of the mountain.

It begins well enough. Wyatt leads Tennessee to a 6-3-1 record in his first year

in 1955 and to a sparkling 10-1-0 record in 1956. That year the Vols are SEC champions and Wyatt is voted National Coach of the Year. Tailback Johnny Majors is a consensus All-America, SEC player of the year, and runner-up for the Heisman Trophy. Among the season's high points is a Vol win over Georgia Tech in a match-up of Neyland disciples Wyatt and Bobby Dodd, members of the fraternity of players-turned-coaches that Neyland produced.

The 1957 team is successful as well, winning eight and losing three. But the long slide into mediocrity begins in 1958 with a 4-6-0 record and continues for Wyatt through 1959 (5-4-1), 1960 (6-2-2), 1961 (6-4-0) and 1962 (4-6-0). He compiles a 49-29-4 record when he is replaced in 1963 by one of his assistant coaches, Jim McDonald. Low points of these last years include a loss in

After relinquishing coaching duties in 1953, Neyland served as UT athletic director, and honoring legends who played for him made for proud occasions. Below, he recognizes Gene McEver for his 1954 induction in the College Football Hall of Fame. With fellow back Buddy Hackman (at rear left), McEver formed the "Hack & Mack" attack that propelled Tennessee to national prominence in 1928.

1958 to small University of Chattanooga at Shields-Watkins Field, resulting in pandemonium as jubilant Chattanooga fans tear down goal posts and engage in a melee broken up by Knoxville fire trucks and police.

There are moments of magic, too. Defending national champion LSU comes to the stadium in 1959 boasting a 19-game winning streak and No. 1 ranking. When the Tigers score a fourth-quarter touchdown to bring them within a point, 14-13, of Tennessee, they elect to go for victory with a two-point conversion attempt. The ball is handed to their powerful, Heisman-winning back, Billy Cannon. He barrels toward the left side of

One of the most gifted and versatile players to don the orange and white, tailback Johnny Majors of Huntland, Tennessee, was named All-America and Heisman Trophy runner-up in 1956 and twice chosen SEC Player of the Year. He returned to his alma mater as coach in 1977 after guiding the University of Pittsburgh to a national championship.

the Tennessee line but is stopped inches shy of the end zone by Billy Majors, Charley Severance and Wayne Grubb. Tennessee's upset victory is preserved, and the image of "The Stop" is permanently placed in the gallery of great Vol moments.

Tennessee also beats favored Auburn in Knoxville in 1959 and defeats both Auburn and Alabama in 1960.

Despite sub-par records, game attendance and fan support are strong enough to warrant another addition to the

For four decades, cartoonist Bill Dyer, who also drew UT game program covers, delighted Knoxville News-Sentinel readers with his artful and whimsical "Dyergrams" illustrating every passing, running and kicking play of a Tennessee game. The 1959 defeat of reigning national champion LSU at Shields-Watkins is depicted by Dyer on the opposite page. At bottom is the goal-line stop of LSU's Billy Cannon to preserve the 14-13 victory.

field. As athletic director, Neyland begins planning a vertical expansion of the stadium that will hide its original brickwork facade behind a towering skirt of metal trusses. By the time the 1962 season arrives, the field boasts an upper deck to the West Stands, adding 5,837 seats and boosting capacity to 52,227. Built atop the deck is an impressive two-story press box that can accommodate 100 reporters as well as special guests of the

University and athletics department.

Neyland never sees the addition completed. He dies March 28, 1962, at the age of 70 of kidney and liver disease while undergoing treatment at Ochsner Foundation Hospital in New Orleans. Even during the final two months of his illness, his enthusiasm for the work in Knoxville is strong as he monitors the weekly progress of the stadium through construction photos sent to his hospital room. A month before he dies,

University trustees vote to name the stadium that has grown up around Shields-Watkins Field in Neyland's honor, a tribute to the man whose program and vision caused its enlargement time and again.

The naming ceremony for Neyland Stadium is held during the Alabama game on October 20, 1962. As a man who keenly appreciated

the value of education, Neyland, in his athletic director's role, quietly directed some funds from his department to academic scholarships at the University. The trustees decide, therefore, to further honor and

continued on page 44

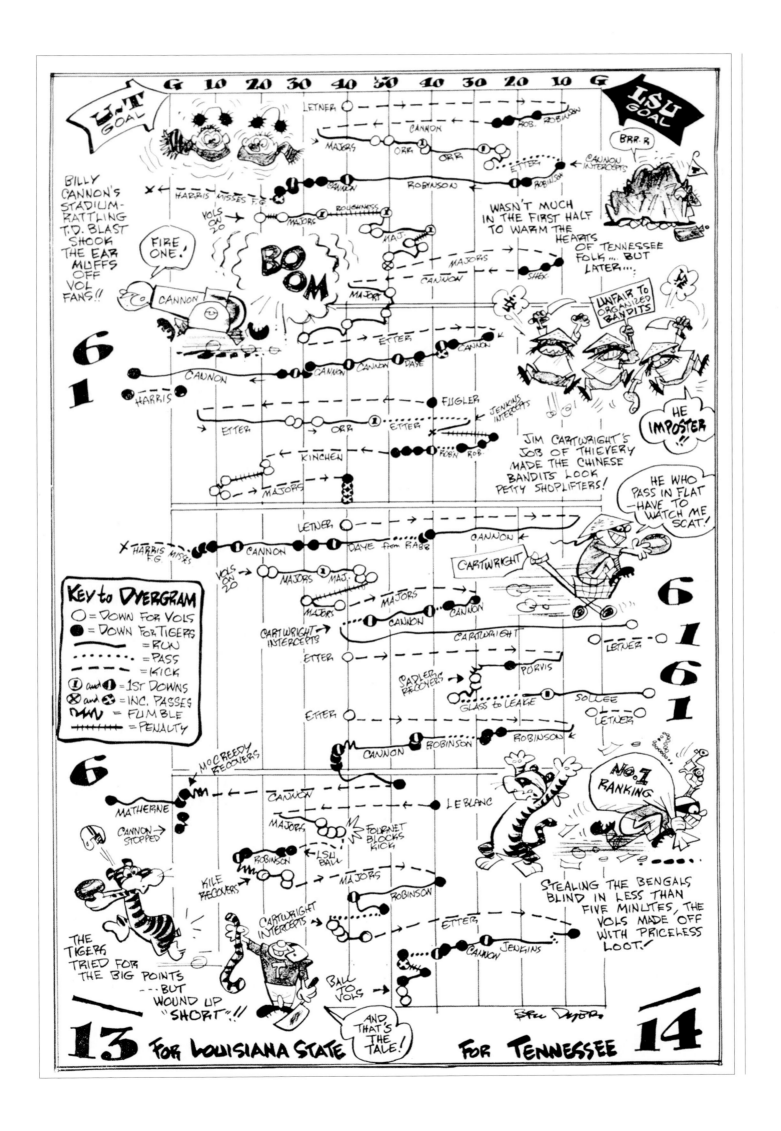

OFFICIAL PROGRAM · FIFTY CENTS

TENNESSEE ALABAMA

OCTOBER 16 · 1954 · SHIELDS-WATKINS FIELD

OFFICIAL PROGRAM · FIFTY CENTS

TENNESSEE VANDERBILT

NOVEMBER 26 · 1953 · SHIELDS-WATKINS FIELD

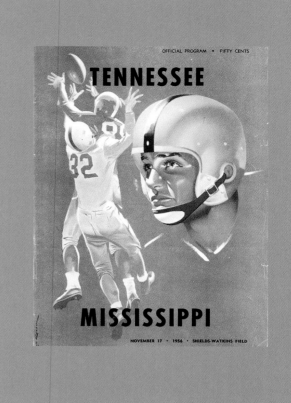

OFFICIAL PROGRAM · FIFTY CENTS

TENNESSEE

MISSISSIPPI

NOVEMBER 17 · 1956 · SHIELDS-WATKINS FIELD

TENNESSEE GEORGIA TECH

NOVEMBER 9 · 1957 · SHIELDS-WATKINS STADIUM

OFFICIAL PROGRAM · FIFTY CENTS

TENNESSEE ★ FLORIDA STATE

OCTOBER 25 · 1958 · SHIELDS-WATKINS FIELD

OFFICIAL PROGRAM · FIFTY CENTS

TENNESSEE ★ OLE MISS.

NOVEMBER 12 · 1960 · SHIELDS-WATKINS FIELD

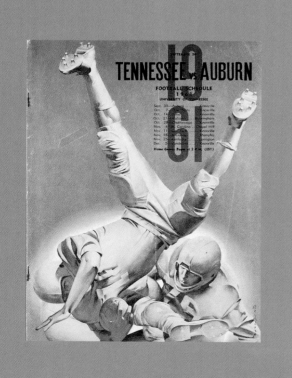

TENNESSEE vs. **AUBURN**

FOOTBALL SCHEDULE
1961
UNIVERSITY OF TENNESSEE

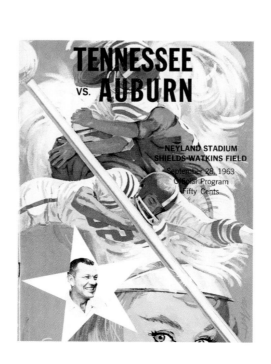

TENNESSEE vs. **AUBURN**

NEYLAND STADIUM
SHIELDS-WATKINS FIELD
September 28, 1963
Official Program
Fifty Cents

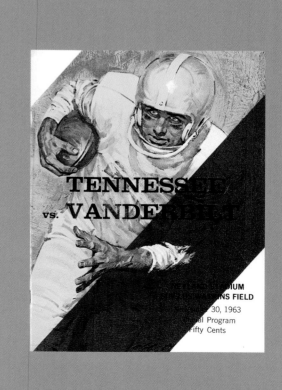

TENNESSEE vs. **VANDERBILT**

NEYLAND STADIUM
SHIELDS-WATKINS FIELD
November 30, 1963
Official Program
Fifty Cents

Neyland Stadium's expansion rested on the shoulders of exciting players like tailback Bill Majors, who carried the ball in the late 1950s, and All-SEC center and linebacker Mike Lucci (snapping to Bunny Orr, left, and Glenn Glass), captain of the 1961 team and a 12-year veteran of the Cleveland Bowns and Detroit Lions. The West Upper Deck rises in 1962, the year Robert Neyland died and the stadium was named in his memory. Following spread: Checkerboard end zones were a new feature of Neyland Stadium when the Vols played Alabama in 1964.

41

"I feel like the Christians must have felt

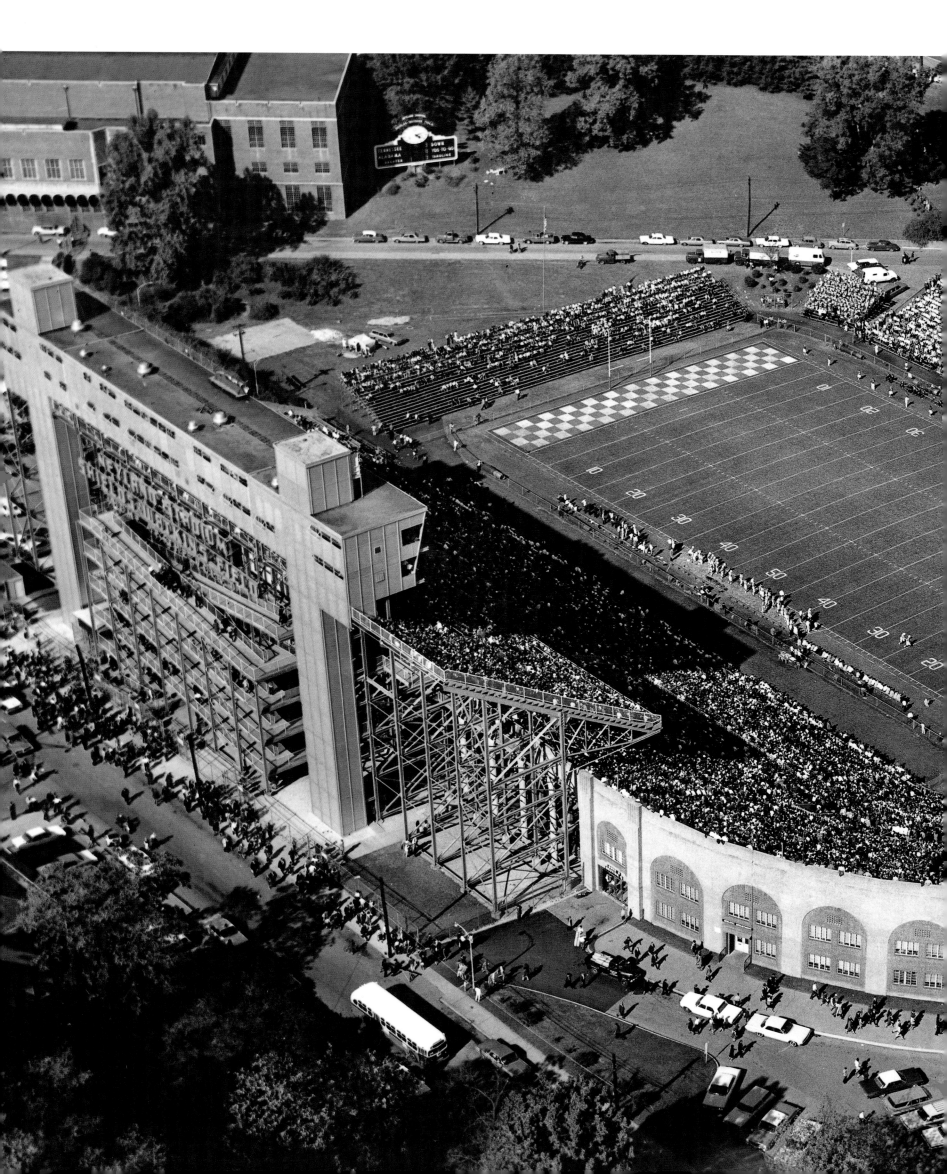

before they let the lions out."

Tulane head coach Jim Pittman before facing the No. 2-ranked Vols on UT homecoming day, 1967

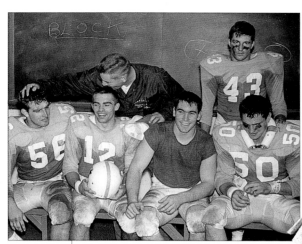

memorialize him by creating a prestigious academic scholarship in his name. In a solicitation never repeated at the stadium, 250 coeds pass containers among the crowd, which contributes more than $10,000 that day toward a $100,000 scholarship endowment. Both the stadium and academic scholarship carry the name and legacy of a larger-than-life figure.

44

Doug Dickey (opposite page, with quarterbacks Bobby Scott, left, and Bubba Wyche) guided the Vols to two SEC championships as head coach from 1964 through 1969. The East Upper Deck was completed; artificial turf, dubbed "Doug's Rug," was placed on the field; UT wingback Lester McClain (following page) broke the SEC football color barrier; and John Ward (at bottom) began a 31-year stint as "Voice of the Vols:" all in 1968. Ward's novel introduction to Vol football occurred when he was six and watched his father, Herschel, principal of Tennessee School for the Deaf in Knoxville, relate UT games to his dormitory students by drawing the ball's movement on a lined-off blackboard as he listened to the play-by-play on the radio.

Jim McDonald, an assistant on Wyatt's coaching staff for seven years, guides the Volunteers in 1963, replacing the single-wing offense of Neyland and Wyatt with the T formation. In compiling a 5-5 record, his team wins four of its final five games, three by shutouts. McDonald will serve as assistant athletic director at UT from 1964 to 1982.

Bob Woodruff, an outstanding Vol tackle for Neyland in the late 1930s and later head coach at Baylor and Florida, accepts the athletic director post at UT in 1963. Soon after returning to his alma mater, Woodruff recruits a new football coach for

the Vols. He's 31-year-old Doug Dickey, who played for Woodruff at Florida in the early 1950s and was a top assistant to coach Frank

Broyles at Arkansas. In his first year in Knoxville in 1964, Dickey's Volunteers post a 4-5-1 record, but hopes are high as his competitive team loses narrowly to Auburn and Alabama, ties LSU in Baton Rouge and upsets Georgia Tech at Grant Field in Atlanta. Middle guard Steve DeLong wins the Outland Trophy and a strong recruiting class includes wide receiver Richmond Flowers, the first of a number of track-football athletes at UT.

A watershed year for the program is

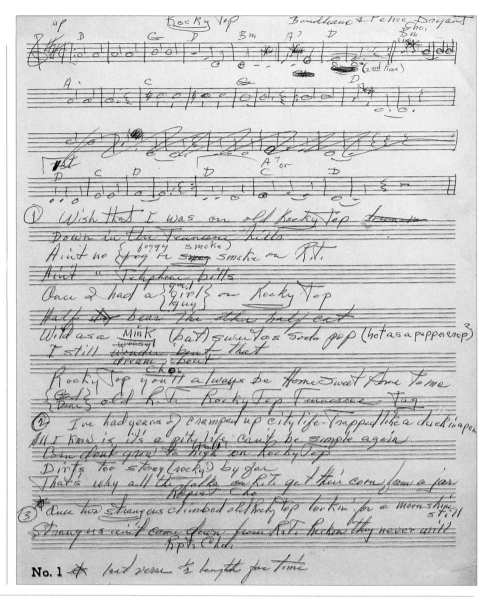

1965, as Tennessee doubles the previous year's victories, finishing 8-1-2. A post-season win over Tulsa in the Bluebonnet Bowl marks the Volunteers' first bowl appearance since 1957. Dickey's teams are off to a sterling string of seasons: 8-3-0 in 1966, 9-2-0 in 1967, 8-2-1 in 1968 and 9-2-0 in 1969. The 1967 season is particularly sweet as Tennessee defeats Alabama for the first time in seven years and Mississippi for the first time in nine, claims the SEC championship, receives the national championship designation by Litkenhous and finishes second in the consensus national poll.

Dickey not only brings consistent winning football back to Tennessee; he and Woodruff help create a new level of excitement in the program. Dickey adds such flourishes as a bold "T" on the side of helmets, the checkerboarding of end zones in orange and white, and the running by players onto the field through the human "T" formed by the band. The "Big Orange

"70,000 screaming fans and I *never* heard a sound."

All-SEC fullback Curt Watson '71, describing the focus-induced silence he experienced until hitting the ground at the end of a play.

Country" slogan takes hold in the region as Vol jackets, caps, pennants and bumper stickers are seen everywhere. Season tickets soar after the 1965 season, and average Neyland attendance surges, from 38,150 in 1964 to 62,120 in 1968.

Helping fuel the phenomenon are a pent-

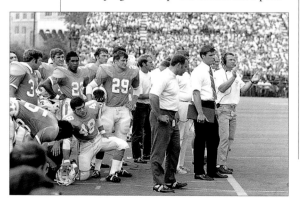

With the arrival of the '70s came the coaching tenure of Bill Battle (59-22-2, from 1970 through 1976); the running of fullback Curt Watson and passing of quarterback Condredge Holloway; the first Neyland night game, a 28-21 victory over Penn State in 1972; and the introduction (and speedy adoption) of "Rocky Top" as UT's fight song, during a 1972 halftime show. Following spread: Celebrating Larry Seivers' game-winning catch against Clemson in 1974 was Gus Manning, briefcase in hand, then UT's Athletic Department business manager.

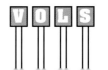

up demand for dominating Vol teams, a growing population of students and alumni to attend games, development of interstate corridors that make reaching Knoxville easier, and the stadium itself — imposing with its large stands, decks and sweeping boxes high above the field. Tennessee has reached a point where the spectacle of game day at Neyland, rich in sounds and sights, transcends the caliber of the opponent. Vol football is no longer a game but a happening.

During this period, UT nurtures a steady stream of football talent. Consensus All-America selections are linebacker Frank Emanuel (1965), linebacker Paul Naumoff (1966), center Bob Johnson (1967), guard Charles Rosenfelder (1968), linebacker Steve

Kiner (1968, 1969), and guard Chip Kell (1969, 1970). Responding to public enthusiasm for the Vols, trustees approve two stadium projects just two years apart: construction of the North Stands in 1966, adding 5,895 seats, and of the East Upper Deck in 1968, adding 6,307 seats. Together, they bring Neyland's capacity to 64,429. The new North Stands, which fills the last open corner of the field, is built bleacher-style and not curved to form a true bowl, which will come 14 years later. A new scoreboard at the north end features a countdown clock, replacing a real clock with minute and second hands.

Besides the East Upper Deck, Neyland Stadium sports a new playing surface in 1968. During the summer, crews working with road-building machines scrape away Shields-Watkins' carefully tended sod and replace it with a paved surface overlaid with an artificial grass carpet called Tartan Turf. It and other synthetic successors will cover the field the next 27 years. The novelty of the surface, the match-up with Georgia (the first time the two schools have played in 31 years) and the presence on the field of Tennessee's first black player, Lester McClain, brings ABC television to Neyland Stadium to broadcast the season-opening 1968 game and *Sports Illustrated* to cover it.

No one is disappointed by the outcome. Behind 17-9 with a minute left in the game, UT roars back. Quarterback Bubba Wyche

50

marches his team 80 yards and hits end Gary Kreis with a touchdown pass as time expires. With zeroes on the clock, Wyche delivers a successful, two-point conversion pass to tight end Kenny DeLong to earn an exciting tie.

Broadcasting the game from the press box over the statewide Vol Network is a new twosome: play-by-play announcer John Ward and his partner, color analyst Bill Anderson. A graduate of UT and the UT law school, Ward is already a recognizable voice to sports fans from his coverage of UT basketball games. Anderson was co-captain of the Vols' 1957 football team and an All-Pro receiver for the Washington Redskins and Green Bay Packers. Over the next 31 years, Ward and Anderson become one of collegiate sports' most celebrated and admired broadcasting teams, known for their knowledge of the game, eminent fairness to both teams on the field, and level of game-calling excitement that thrills hundreds of thousands of Vol fans from populous cities to remote corners of the state. Ward's trademark exclamation, "Give him six! Touchdown, Tennessee," finds a sweet spot in the Vol vernacular.

They follow UT broadcasters Pat Roddy, Jr., Joe Epstein, Mel Levitt, Lowell Blanchard, Lindsey Nelson, who gains national fame as

sportscaster, and George Mooney. When Ward and Anderson step down at the end of the 1998 national championship season, the mike is passed to Bob Kesling who works in the Neyland booth with ana-

players. With one of the largest audiences for a program of its type in the nation, the Saturday Vol Radio Network broadcast is regarded as radio sports at its visceral best.

In Dickey's last year as Vol coach in 1969, his team posts a 9-2-0 record and wins the SEC championship. Joy turns to dismay at season's end when he announces his departure to coach for his alma mater, Florida, in a region where he has family ties. During his six-year stay at UT, he compiles a 46-15-4 record, twice wins the conference championship and re-energizes the program. He will return to UT 16 years later, in 1985, to succeed Bob Woodruff as athletic director.

Dickey's successor is 28-year-old assistant UT coach Bill Battle, who takes the reins of the powerful Vols as the youngest college coach in the nation and enjoys immediate success. In his first year, 1970, Tennessee is 11-1-0, including a Sugar Bowl victory over Air Force, making Battle the first NCAA Division I coach to win 11 games his first year. Vol fans relish a come-from-behind victory over UCLA that season and Neyland Stadium wins in successive weeks over Alabama, with Battle opposing his former coach, Paul "Bear" Bryant, and Dickey-coached Florida.

While Johnny Majors was coaching the likes of (from left) Tony Robinson, Daryl Dickey and Randy Sanders, Doug Dickey was returning to UT as athletic director in 1985, here receiving congratulations from son, Daryl, who quarterbacked Tennessee to an SEC championship that season and a stirring, 35-7 defeat of heavily-favored Miami in the Sugar Bowl. In 1987, the stadium acquired a new press box and executive suites and a fresh carpet of synthetic turf.

lysts Tim Priest and Jeff Francis. They convey to those unable to sit in Neyland the experience of a day at the stadium, from pregame chatter, to the unfolding of plays on the field, to post-game interviews with coaches and

Tennessee earns impressive 10-2-0 records in 1971, with defensive back Bobby Majors a consensus All-America, and 1972. The Southwest Upper Deck atop the rounded horseshoe portion of the stadium is built in time for the 1972 season, adding 6,221 seats and bringing the stadium's capacity to 70,650. At the same time, banks of lights are erected above the east and west stands so fans can enjoy late summer games in the relative coolness of evening. Neyland hosts its first night game September 16, 1972, against Penn State, a team Tennessee defeated the year before to snap a Nittany Lions 15-game win streak. Led by quarterback Condredge Holloway, dubbed "The Artful Dodger" for his break-away running style, UT wins again, 28-21, before a record, standing-room-only crowd of 71,622 and a national television audience.

As it happens, the Vols won't see another 10-win season for 15 years. During the last four years of Battle's tenure, UT's record gradually declines: 8-4-0 in 1973, 7-3-2 in 1974, 7-5-0 in 1975 and 6-5-0 in 1976. Fans grow impatient with mounting losses, particularly to Alabama and Auburn. They don't show their displeasure by avoiding Neyland, however. In 1975, the stadium draws over half a million (507,677) for the first time. One of the most exciting players of the era is sure-fingered wide-receiver Larry Seivers, a consensus All-America in 1975 and 1976.

As season ticket sales continue to grow, UT trustees approve construction of the Southeast Upper Deck, adding 9,600 seats and bringing capacity to 80,250 for the debut of the 1976 season. A record crowd of 82,687 (first ever over 80,000 at Neyland) watches the Vols lose the opening game to Duke. After the team loses to Alabama and stumbles against Kentucky, Battle steps down as coach. But Neyland attendance for the frustrating year is above capacity: 80,703.

Tennessee fans hail the return of favorite son Johnny Majors as coach, in 1977. As a Vol player, the Huntland native and member of a legendary Tennessee football family was an All-America tailback, twice SEC Player of the Year and the 1956 Heisman Trophy runner-up for coach Bowden Wyatt. He is lured to UT from Pittsburgh where he coached the Panthers to the 1976 national title behind the running of Tony Dorsett and was named National Coach of the Year. With Vol fans clamoring for Majors as Battle's replacement, UT Chancellor Jack Reese announces the school's ordained decision in tongue-in-cheek fashion. "After an extensive nationwide search," he begins, drawing laughter at a large press conference introducing the new coach. The strains of "When Johnny Comes Marching Home" are heard across Big Orange Country.

Quick success, however, will not follow Majors to Tennessee. In his first three seasons, 1977 through 1979, his record is below .500 at 16-17-1. It will not be until the eighth year of his 15-year UT coaching career that he fields an SEC champion and his tenth year that he wins 10 games. The Vols' erratic early performance is exemplified by back-to-back games at Neyland in 1979. They are embarrassed by underdog Rutgers 23-7 (before the matchup, a local sportswriter asks about the lightly regarded eastern team: "What's a Rutgers?"), but the following week Tennessee whips nationally ranked Notre Dame 40-28 before a howling, intimidating crowd of 86,489.

Tennessee's ability to play memorable football on any given Saturday keeps sold-out crowds attending Neyland games, watching the likes of consensus All-America back Roland James perform. In 1979, season ticket sales soar past 50,000, and a successful fund-raising campaign is conducted to finance a $7 million addition to the stadium. The construction of a curved north end to replace the north stands and Section X creates a mammoth bowl.

Completed by the start of the 1980 season, the project adds 10,499 seats, increasing capacity to 91,249 and making Neyland the second largest on-campus college football venue (after Michigan Stadium) in the nation.

The first Neyland crowd to exceed 90,000 (95,288) attends the opening game of the season as Georgia defeats Tennessee 16-15 en route to a national championship. A dream, seven-game home schedule that includes Southern California, Alabama and Pittsburgh produces an average Neyland game attendance of 94,170

53

despite a 5-6-0 record for the season.

Consistency improves from 1981 through 1986 as the Vols produce a combined 46-22-4 record and win the SEC championship in 1985. One of this period's most memorable Neyland games occurs on October 16, 1982, as UT defeats No. 2-ranked, heavily-favored Alabama 35-28, ending Alabama's 11-year win streak over the Vols. Goal posts come down and players already undressing in the locker room put their jerseys back on and return to the field for a standing ovation from a deliriously happy crowd. Majors is carried by his players across the field to accept the congratulations of Coach Bryant, who is making his final appearance at the stadium. The legendary coach resigns after the season and dies the following January.

Defensive tackle Reggie White captains the Vols to a 9-3-0 record in 1983 and offensive guard Bill Mayo is a standout on a 1984 team that is 7-4-1. Both are consensus All-America choices, as is wide receiver Tim McGee, in 1985. UT beats No. 1-ranked Auburn 38-20 at Neyland that year on the way to a 9-1-2 record and the Vols' first SEC championship since 1969. The Vols clinch the conference title with a 30-0 win over Vanderbilt in the season finale before a record crowd of 97,372.

Anticipating a banner year, 73,801 attend the spring 1986 Orange and White intersquad game in a record display of collegiate preseason excitement and support. The team is 7-5-0 that fall, but the following year, 1987, improves to 10-2-1. The press box, perched above the west stands like a building on stilts, is expanded to four floors in time for the season. It contains box seats for guests of the University and athletics department, leased

suites, and facilities for print and broadcast media. The press box will later be named for Tom Elam, long-time UT trustee and Athletics Board member, and the print and broadcast levels for John Ward, whose honors include Collegiate Broadcaster of the Year.

A 5-6-0 record in 1988 is earned only by winning five of the season's last six games. But that momentum carries to the first of three successful years that follow. The Vols boast the most improved record in the country by winning 11 and losing one in 1989 and sharing the SEC championship. Reggie Cobb and Chuck Webb form a powerful backfield tandem and guard Eric Still is a consensus All-America.

The team is 9-2-2 in 1990, winning the SEC championship outright. Among victories is a 45-3 trouncing of Florida at Neyland. The Vols have another strong year in 1991, finishing 9-3-0. Defensive back Dale Carter is a consensus All-America that year, as is tackle Antone Davis the year before.

In 1992, perhaps the program's most controversy-ridden year, Majors resigns and assistant coach Phillip Fulmer takes his place. The season begins with Majors in the hospital convalescing from heart surgery. As interim coach, Fulmer guides the Vols to three victories, including impressive back-to-back wins over 14th-ranked Georgia, 34-31, and fourth-ranked Florida, 31-14. Majors returns to the sidelines, and the Vols lose three games in October. He announces his resignation a month later,

Phillip Fulmer became UT's head coach at the close of the 1992 season and gained his first 50 victories quicker than any SEC coach in history. Helping him achieve that record was quarterback Peyton Manning (1994-1997), who won the Sullivan Award as the nation's top amateur athlete and, like predecessor Heath Shuler, was runner-up for the Heisman Trophy. Artificial turf was removed at the end of the 1993 season, and the field was planted in grass requiring 4,000 bushels of sprigs. Construction of the North Upper Deck in 1996 completed double-decking of the bowl.

55

VOLS

Docking of the Vol Navy near Neyland Stadium on the Tennessee River (contrasted with a similar mooring of boats in 1959) and the Pride of the Southland band's pre-game "Salute To The Hill" have become part of game-day pageantry. Quarterback Tee Martin, opposite page, helped add a lustrous chapter to Vol football history by leading the 1998 team to a 13-0 season including an overtime defeat of Florida that brought down the Neyland house.

and Fulmer is named the team's new head coach. The season ends 9-3-0 with a Hall of Fame Bowl victory over Boston College.

Fulmer, who played offensive guard for the Vols from 1969 through 1971, fashions a storybook run of seasons as coach. The Vols finish second in the SEC East with a 10-2-0 record in 1993 as quarterback Heath Shuler is selected runner-up for the Heisman Trophy. Tennessee blisters Vanderbilt 62-14 in the final home game of the year and the last on Neyland's artificial turf, which has covered

the field since 1968. As soon as the season ends, crews begin pulling up the carpet and cutting it into small squares that are sold to fans as mementos for offices and homes.

The field is sprigged with Bermuda grass the following summer in an $800,000 project that is planned and directed with the precision of a football campaign. The all-Tennessee turf built in layers upon the field's subsoil requires 4,000 bushels of sprigs from Fayetteville, sand from Rogersville, and a base of pea gravel from the nearby

Tennessee River. Cherry laurel bushes that will mature into sideline hedges arrive from McMinnville. Buried 30 inches beneath the field are drainage pipes, while high-pressure cannons aimed from the side-lines keep the grass, daily clipped to three-fourths-inch height, well-watered. Ready for the 1994 season is a botanical spectacle: a two-acre play-ing field built to the specifications and manicured to the quality of a U.S. Golfing Association putting green.

The 1994 season begins on a disheart-ening note with an injury to the team's first-string quarterback in the early minutes of the opening game. But the team responds well to adversity. After a 1-3 start, the Vols win seven of their last eight games, including a bowl victory, to end the year with a laudable 8-4 record. They also find in freshman Peyton Manning, son of Ole Miss and New Orleans Saints quarterback Archie Manning, an exceptional passer and team leader.

The Vols achieve a superlative 11-1-0 record in 1995 as Manning, halfback Jay Graham and receiver Joey Kent set school records for passing, rushing and receiving, respectively. Six Neyland crowds exceed 97,000 as average game attendance reaches 96,398 in a stadium built for 91,902. Away games include a rousing victory over Alabama. UT defeats Ohio State 20-14 in the Florida Citrus Bowl to finish the season ranked second in the CNN-USA Today Coaches Poll.

At season's end, work begins on the Upper Deck of the North End of the stadium. It completes the bowl's double decking, adding 10,642 seats and bringing capacity to 102,544 for the start of the 1996 season. Those familiar with the Neyland phenome-non know a built seat is a filled seat, and the season confirms this as attendance routinely exceeds capacity by 3,000 or more. A colle-giate-record crowd of 107,608 attends a rainy September 21 clash with Florida. Though spirits are dampened by the outcome, fans are cheered by a come-from-behind 20-13 victory in October over Alabama and an overall 10-2-0 record and Top-10 national ranking for the second consecutive year.

The best is still to come. Senior Peyton Manning leads the Vols to an 11-2 record in

1997 and their first SEC championship in seven years. An outside chance for a national title is ended by a humbling, 42-17 loss to Nebraska in the Orange Bowl. Manning and linebacker Leonard Little are consensus All-Americas, and Manning becomes the most decorated Vol player ever by winning a

clutch of prestigious honors: the Maxwell, Davey O'Brien, Johnny Unitas and Sullivan (to the nation's best amateur athlete) awards, National Scholar-Athlete of the Year, and runner-up in Heisman Trophy balloting. His jersey is retired the following spring during halftime ceremonies at the Orange and White Game.

Fulmer enters the 1998 season having gained his first 50 victories quicker than any SEC coach in history and owning the best winning percentage among active NCAA football coaches with five years experience

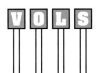

"This national champion is clad in BIG ORANGE; Tennessee 23, Florida State 16."

John Ward's final words of the final game in his 31-year career as "Voice of the Vols"

or more. His team, however, is considered too hurt by the loss of Manning, Little and other starters to contend for the conference title, much less a national championship. Yet, in a season of great per-

formances and surprises, the Vols do just that. The tone is set in the national-ly televised opening game against Syracuse in the Carrier Dome, won by UT 34-33 on a last-second field goal.

Pulling rabbits from a hat becomes routine for the Vols. Against Florida, a missed, 32-yard field goal by Gator place-kicker Collins Cooper enables UT to preserve a 20-17 over-time victory, ending UT's five-year string of defeats to Florida and unloosing a crazed Neyland crowd that shakes the press box with its stomping, tears down the goal posts and gouges chunks from the field. Late in the season at Neyland, UT rallies from a 14-point deficit to defeat Arkansas, 28-24, scoring the winning touchdown

with 28 seconds left in the game. The improbable finish is made possible when Arkansas quarterback Clint Stoerner trips over his feet as he drops back to pass and

fumbles the ball, giving the Vols the gift of a final chance.

In such ways does Tennessee pass 11-0 through the regular season. The Vols defeat Mississippi State, 24-14, for the SEC championship and Florida State, 23-16, in the Fiesta Bowl at Tempe, Arizona, in the first Bowl Championship Series (BCS) matchup. For the second time in the program's rich history and first time in 47 years, the Vols are proclaimed con-sensus national champi-ons (by AP, ESPN/USA Today, Football Writers' Association of America, and National Football Foundation and College Hall of Fame). Quarterback Tee Martin sets the NCAA record for consecutive pass comple-tions during the regular season, linebacker Al Wilson is a consensus All-America and Fulmer is

Tennessee's defeat of Florida State at the Fiesta Bowl in Tempe, Arizona, made the Vols undisputed 1998 National Champions and closed a century in which UT won two consensus national championships (1951 was the other) and shared four more (1938, 1940, 1950, 1967). Members of the 1998 team received a rousing Vol Walk reception (on following spread) in the spring of 1999. Neyland entered the year 2000 with new East Stand skyboxes and the second largest seating capacity (104,079) of any college football stadium in America. The Vols had enjoyed winning home records on Shields-Watkins Field in 72 of the 78 seasons since it was dedicated in 1921.

voted National Coach of the Year. The Vols stand on Rocky Top, surveying their domain.

The year following a perfect, national-championship season is one of the most difficult for a team to approach. The euphoria of winning the trophy is fresh in mind and hopeful talk of a rare repeat is heard. In a climate of high expectations, the Vols achieve an otherwise excellent 9-2 record in 1999 but feel the disappointment of slipping from national championship contention and then losing to Nebraska for the second time in three years in a postseason bowl. Cosey Coleman, Deon Grant and Raynoch Thompson earn All America honors. The 2000 season begins with bright prospects filling the ranks of starters depleted by the NFL draft.

Two impressive structures, meanwhile, are added to the stadium rim. Before the 1999 season begins, a JumboTron scoreboard is mounted to the south end on giant stanchions that crest the bowl, so that the huge electronic scoreboard and replay screen loom above the field. Prior to the 2000 season, towering sky boxes are constructed above the East Stands, balancing the press box and suites above the West Stands. In what becomes the stadium's 15th seating expansion, the east side boxes add 1,250 seats, bringing Neyland's capacity to 104,079. An architectural culmination of Neyland's symmetrical growth has been achieved.

What then has been the harvest from Neyland soil, even as the stadium has risen around it? Of 78 football seasons since Shields-Watkins Field was dedicated in 1921 (no games were played in 1943), the Vols enjoyed winning home records in 72 of them. In 24 of those seasons, the team was perfect at home. In another nine seasons,

only a tie blemished the record. Tennessee legends who have done battle Saturdays in Neyland include 187 who were chosen All-SEC, 73 All-Americas, 30 consensus All-Americas, and 19 College Football Hall of Fame inductees, including two coaches, Neyland and Wyatt. Since attendance records were kept in 1950, more than 20 million fans have attended home games.

The stadium and field are about more than statistics, though. They're about indelible memories. There's the boy who sells out of the soft drinks that he hawks at the game and is allowed to kneel at the side of the end zone late in

The Knoxville News-Sentinel

TUESDAY

FINAL EDITION
www.knoxnews.com

JANUARY 5, 1999
$2.00

SPECIAL TODAY ▶ 16-PAGE FIESTA BOWL SECTION

CHAMPIONS!
Tennessee 23, Florida State 16

Tennessee coach Phillip Fulmer celebrates with quarterback Tee Martin (17) after the Vols defeated Florida State 23-16 in the Fiesta Bowl on Monday to win the National Championship.

INSIDE COVERAGE

Tennessee linebacker Al Wilson gets a hug from defensive coordinator John Chavis after the Vols defeated Florida State on Monday night.

The 47-year wait is over. Vols are
No. 1

By Mike Strange
News-Sentinel sports writer

UT has a new fight song: 'We're No. 1'

JOHN ADAMS
Sports Editor

NHL
Predators beat Mighty Ducks, 2-1
Page 8C

SPORTS

THE TENNESSEAN

TUESDAY, JANUARY 5, 1999

VOLUNTEERS (13-0) ARE NATI

Rocky
Of The

Tennessee wide receiver Peerless Price runs with a reception from Tee Martin to complete a 79-yard touchdown play in the fourth quarter

UT drops Florida State, 23

By Chris Low / Sports Writer

TEMPE, Ariz. — All season long, they were the team that couldn' never-say-die Tennessee Vols. Last night, in the crisp, cool air of the Sun, they were the best team in the country. Period.

---

the second half where he has the best view in the house of the "The Stop" of Billy Cannon. He lives in South Carolina now, but the image summons him to Neyland year after year. There's great Vol fullback Curt Watson remembering the sound of silence on the field in his playing days. His concen-

tration while he waits for the ball filters out the roar of the crowd; he claims to hear it only when unpiling at the end of a play.

There are a million memories that combine to form what Vol writer Tom Mattingly calls the mystique of the stadium: all those ghosts of great plays and players, coaches and rivalries palpably felt on the empty

field. Bob Campbell, director of grounds and maintenance for the athletic department, had an eerie feeling when he grasped a solid piece of memory, a section of drainage pipe that was placed under the field 60 years ago and unearthed when grass was replanted six years back.

In contemporary appearance, the stadium has become a celebrity. Its orange-and-white checkerboard end zones are recognized across the country. TV viewers see Neyland lit and spinning like a jewel on a clear Knoxville night from the rotating camera of a blimp. On rainy days when orange ponchos in the stands are plentiful, the huge bowl is awash in bright color, looking strangely festive under leaden skies. Perfect in form and always filled to capacity, it's an enthralling sight. Travelers along I-40 who aren't Vol fans at all will drive by the campus for a look, drawn by the gravity of Neyland's size and spectacle.

But the pull on fans is more intimate. "I grew up listening to the games on the radio," says Campbell, "and I can still locate the seats where we later sat. It becomes part of your life. Look at what it's meant to people over so much time.

"This field," he declares, "is bigger than a property deed. It's not yours; it's not mine; it's not the football team's. No one owns it.

61

GAME DAY

`8:00 am` Steam begins to warm the 200 wieners nestled inside the shiny, stainless-steel push cart parked on the sidewalk outside the northwest corner of Neyland Stadium. Red and yellow squeeze-bottles of condiments line the rack. It's four hours before kickoff, the first bag of buns is yet to be broken and the first whiff of mustard and relish to flavor the air, but already vendor Johnny Sunday can see them coming.

He can visualize the milling throng of orange-clad fans that will build from a trickle to a wave that rolls across the grounds of the stadium, engulfing him and everything before it hours before a referee blows a whistle and drops an arm to start the game. All but deserted now in the fluttering, cool breeze of a quiet Saturday morning, the stadium's drive will soon become the most densely packed artery in the South.

Already, they're coming, rising at the groggy crack of dawn from towns in Tennessee and Georgia and the Carolinas, barreling down I-81 and I-75 and I-40, racing to Knoxville on coffee and adrenalin. They meticulously arrange their hats and pennants and pom-poms and cushions in rear windows, while orange windsocks and flags snap in the draft of their cars. They stream toward the stadium linked in common purpose like a cavalry troop, colors flying, charging to a fight.

Fences open and cordons drop as parking lots near the stadium accept the first arrivals. Cars and campers find their slots, as do orange-fringed boats on the river, and the communal love-in begins. They're a chatty group that welcomes newcomers with hugs and hearty greetings and proffered food. Coolers are opened, sandwiches handed out. Smiling orange is everywhere. It's football time in Tennessee, and on this bright, rich-with-promise morning, there's no better place on earth to be.

`9:00 am` Inside the empty cathedral, the sound system is checked. Sitting 50 feet apart on the concrete walks that border the length of the field are five-foot-high black speakers angled up at the stands. Suddenly, "Get Back, Jack" blares with rock-concert amperage. When it's over and the reverberation dies, the speakers continue to hiss quietly with life. Two engineers check the public address system. "One, two, hey, wha, wha. One, two, ha, ha," goes

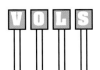

the drill from the press box mike. "How's the vocal in the end zone, Tony?" one of them asks. "It's fine," says his partner. "It's kickin' butt."

It is tomb-like in the high-ceilinged, fluorescent-lit home-team locker room under the north stands: an intense quiet that speaks of pregame nerves. The players are yet to arrive, but you can see the tenseness in the eyes

of orange-cushioned chairs, ten to a row, face a blackboard where coaches diagram, lecture and exhort. Painted in orange on a white cinderblock wall of the room are General Robert Neyland's seven commandments of winning:

"The team that makes the fewest mistakes will win...Play for and make the breaks and when one comes your way, SCORE...If at first the game, or breaks, go

and jaws of trainers and equipment handlers, in their spare words and fussy concerns, as they ready everything for the dressing and taping ritual that lies 60 minutes ahead.

At each player's open cubicle, shoulder pads hang from a wooden peg. The pads have copper grommets in the waist belt and leather cords to cinch at the chest — the armament of gladiators. A helmet rests on a jersey draped neatly over each player's bench. Next to each helmet are a pair of orange gloves, an orange mouth guard, and a stick of gum. A pair of shoes is lined up on the carpeted floor before each stall: three pairs for the punters. The day's game guide rests on each bench.

Throughout the dressing room, names of Tennessee All-America and All-SEC players are inscribed on orange plaques. Here's your lineage, they seem to be saying, carry on the tradition.

Next door in the team meeting room, nine rows

against you, don't let up; put on more steam...Protect our kickers, our quarterback, our lead and our ball game...Cover, block, cut and slice, pursue and gang tackle, for this is the WINNING EDGE...Press the kicking game; here's where the breaks are made...Carry the fight to our opponent and keep it there for 60 minutes." By the time they leave the program, most players will know the maxims by heart, for life.

9:50 am More than two hours before game time, fans sit, stand and squat on every inch of shaded space on a grassy slope beyond the northwest corner of the stadium. From a platform at the bottom of the lawn-cum-amphitheater, UT's play-by-play announcer and color analysts sign autographs and pose with families for pictures. Then they don earphones as the

claps and cheers. The team disappears inside the stadium, bound for the locker room. The crowd, parted for a moment, closes back in. Amid the bobbing ocean of orange that now fills streets, parking lots, plazas and knolls, Johnny Sunday's cart can barely be seen. He's 85 wieners down, and you can slice the smell of kraut and mustard and relish in the air.

Vol Radio Network's pregame Kick-off Call-in Show goes live on the air. Fielding questions from listeners as the buzz of the crowd swirls about them, they broadcast the charged atmosphere of game-day to corporate towers and country stores, barber shops and backyard barbecues — to a million fans — across the state.

The University's "Pride of the Southland Marching Band," 320-strong, rounds the corner of the drive in its pregame march to the stadium. A dozen whirling batons tossed high in the air and the white plumes of musicians' tall, visored hats can be seen above spectators massed along the street. Others jam a pedestrian bridge and line the stadium's six levels of ramps for a clear view of the spectacle. The punch of the flaring sousaphones, the blare of the brass, the martial spirit of the drum corps quicken the pulse. When "Rocky Top" is played, the clapping crowd roars with approval.

Emotions are no less strong along the avenue that leads from Gibbs Hall, the athletic dorm, to the stadium's west entrance. Coaches and players, dressed in slacks and blazers, make the "Vol Walk" behind the flashing blue lights of a police motorcycle escort. A throng lines the street, heads craning for a look at team members wearing dead-ahead game-face expressions. A pep band plays "Rocky Top," and everyone

10:15 am Inside the stadium, the grounds crew paints last-minute markings on end zones that were checkered orange and white two days before. Grass on the playing field is groomed to a low, thick carpet of Bermuda and rye. Cheerleaders' megaphones are lined against the green link fence and laurel hedge that bound the field. Ushers in orange shirts and teal vests huddle for instructions at entrance tunnels around the double-decked bowl. The big speakers pick up chatter in the PA booth in the sweeping press box that rides high above the stadium, as imposing in its jut as the bridge of an ocean liner.

Visiting players in warm-ups amble from their dressing room beneath the south stands, through the ground-level tunnel, onto the field. They stand at the apex of an inverted ziggurat that climbs and recedes before them in terraced rows of more than 100,000 seats. They walk the crown of the field, taking in the sight lines, the sounds and the space. A national sports network tapes a banner to a concrete wall near the end zone. The stadium's electronic signs flash messages to the nearly 30,000 already in the stands: **"Practice good sportsmanship...Remember UT's reputation for friendliness toward our visitors... Welcome to Neyland Stadium, Home of the Vols."**

`11:00am` **Place kicks boom like muffled cannon fire as they sail end-over-end through the north stands goal post.** Quarterbacks lob warm-up tosses to receivers. A perfect spiral of a punt floats against the deep-blue sky. Flag bearers and majorettes mass beneath the stands at the northwest edge of the field. A cheerleader, held horizontally at the waist in a two-arm press, videotapes her teammates below. The Volunteer paces the sidelines in brown buckskin pants and jacket and coonskin hat. Held on a leash and wearing an orange blanket bearing his name, Smokey sniffs the air. "Rocky Top" is heard for the first time inside the stadium, and the crowd continues to grow.

Both teams are on the field, running their light stretch-

ing, passing and blocking drills 20 yards apart. Edgy coaches move among the players. Reacting to the left or right flick of a coach's finger, hulking linemen move laterally in the cross-over, synchronized step of a chorus line. Players secure each other's helmets, one hand pushing down on the helmet, the other on a teammate's shoulder pads for leverage, in a confiding-like embrace. A cameraman gets a ground-level shot of players stretching their hamstrings for footage at the top of a national telecast.

"You guys picked the right day," says smiling defensive ends coach Steve Caldwell to a group of high school prospects and their parents standing in the north end zone. They watch the players continue their warm-ups as the vast, swept-back stadium fills beneath a sun-drenched sky. **"If you can't get ready to play in this place, you can't get ready to play,"** he says with a broader smile. "You guys enjoy the day."

`11:45am` An orange awning with "T" printed on it extends a few yards from the north stands to the edge of the field. After touching their fingertips to a painted message above the locker room exit pledging, "I will give my all for Tennessee today," players will follow a 30-foot orange carpet until they reach the awning and run onto the field. But the Pride of the Southland band has yet to form its double-lined "T" and for now, two referees stand under the awning and cast their eyes about the stadium filling to distant top rows where standing-room-only

game, and awaken us to the greater purpose of our lives." Bitzas sings the "Star Spangled Banner" with operatic richness and flourish, ending the last verse by lifting his voice in a high-note crescendo that thrills the crowd.

As "Rocky Top" is played and the band forms the Power "T," one-hundred-thousand-plus roar as one —

spectators will line the wall.

As he has for years, public address announcer Bobby Denton describes items for sale at Neyland and closes with the familiar refrain: "We urge you to pay these prices AND PLEASE PAY NO MORE!" — his emphasis on the last five words inviting a gleeful chorus to join him from the stands. As he has for years, George Bitzas stands on the west side of the field with a cordless mike and pitch pipe in his hands, warming his vocal chords by singing in sotto voce the national anthem.

Suddenly, drumsticks clack and the fuse is lit. Signaled to their feet by the sound, the crowd rises with a lusty yell. To the pulse of toms and snares and base drums, the band uncurls from the sidelines into field formation. Six tossed cheerleaders spin into their catchers' arms. The band plays the fight song of the opponent whose school flag, in an elevated gesture, moves ahead of the 12 SEC school colors that cross the length of the field. The spangle-jacketed girls of the color guard snap their silk flags in smart, squared-off moves. Bare-shouldered majorettes prance in sequined outfits, sunlight flashing on their bodices. Fans stand and cheer.

The invocation is given: "Almighty God, we ask by your grace that fans and players alike experience true sportsmanship. Keep our play wholly (cleverly inserted or unintended, this sounds like "holy") within the rules of the

a sound that doesn't build as it would in a smaller, open stadium, but ignites in the bowl with percussive force.
The standing crowd claps rhythmically as the Volunteer with his flag, Smokey with his handlers and a squad of tumbling cheerleaders run, as if catapulted, through the base of the "T," followed on their heels by the team. Like Bitzas, the crowd seems to find a new range for its voice. "Noise," "Get Louder," urge flashing signs in the stadium, as if anyone needs the prompt. The place-kicker awaits the signal that starts the game. Cheerleaders, with perfect VOLS painted on perfect cheeks, watch from the sidelines. To the faithful, this is the perfect place to be.

`12:00PM` A red, rubber kicking tee sails a few bumpy yards as contact is made and the ball it cradled is lofted on its long, spinning downfield trajectory. **"Here we go," says an excited grounds crew member, making a last-second adjustment to a red pylon at the corner of an end zone. "Not a better place for football in the world."**

At the bottom level of the press box, Vol broadcasters and their spotters lean forward at a table placed before an open window perched over the 50-yard line within shoulder-tapping distance of back-row fans and four sto-

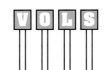

ries above the playing field. The foam bubbles of microphone headsets rest an inch from their lips, and every syllable they utter is instant cause for whoops or groans across the state.

A level above, it's quiet as an operating room. Reporters sit with lap-top computers at three tiers of tables before a wide, hermetically-sealed, solid-glass view

of the field. Ceiling-mounted TV sets show the game but are turned to mute. A UT announcer in the booth calls each play's result in a monotone while another staffer keys it on a computer, creating an official, running fact-sheet that will be handed to the press. Professional restraint is the law of this box. Contesting emotions are checked at the door; audible expressions can get you expelled. Still, there are a few whispered groans and curses when a Vol receiver drops a wide-open pass. "Damn," mutters a writer as he leans toward a colleague, "that was a TD for sure."

There's no such restraint in the stands, no glass and walls and rules to curb you. Salvos of screams and cheers burst in the air. "Yeaaahhh!" goes the crowd, anticipating a long, break-away run. "Oooohhh," goes their disappointment when a shoestring tackle is made. **As Tennessee drives, emotions build. Stomping their feet in unison, fans produce a tremor in the stands. The concrete shivers beneath them.**

Cheerleaders bark through megaphones, pom-poms shake furiously, sound and energy mount in swells. A play at the goal line lifts everyone to their feet. The score ignites a thunderous roar and a crackle of fireworks that lingers in ragged plumes of smoke above the southeast stands.

Not fifteen minutes later during another goal-line play,

the crowd grows hushed. Diving for the end zone, a Vol running back hits a wall of defenders at the scrimmage line, jackknifes in mid air and plummets head-first to the ground. There's a gasp from the crowd and dead silence, as if a plug has been pulled. The player lies motionless as physicians run on the field. His teammates stand near, helmets in hand, nervously eyeing him. The opposing team keeps its vigil at a respectful distance. Barely a word is spoken in the stands. The "P" word hangs in the air. You can hear the drone of a plane.

A green and yellow injury cart drives to the goal line. There's applause as the fallen player is gently lifted aboard on a stretcher. He's fully conscious, at least, and there's movement in his arms. As he disappears in the tunnel, there lingers a cloud of concern on this cloudless day. But the game will go on. Tennessee scores on the very next play. The crowd whoops. Band members shimmy in their seats. "Rocky Top" is played. Twenty-five minutes later comes the PA announcement that the player can move all his limbs and will undergo a scan. Neyland rocks.

So goes a game's ebb and flow, jubilation and consternation as twin companions. **To be a Vol fan at Neyland is to feel the gamut of emotion, but it's also to know that over a home season, there will almost certainly be more joy than heartbreak, more laughter than tears, more victory than defeat.** Plays are run, quarters tick away and the sun passes over the bowl. Outside the stadium, it's nearly deserted. Johnny Sunday's push cart is gone. Single-engine pipers trail long, retail messages as they fly above the stands. Then comes another banner: "Happy Anniversary, Lisa. I love you. Scott." You can imagine one couple embracing at that moment, no matter what's happening on the field. UT wins, and love is in the air.

`3:45PM` It's the final home game of the year, a division has been won and celebration is in full swing. Players take turns running the length of the field with the huge, flowing Tennessee flag in tow. "Congratulate

hum of the speakers can be heard again. Everywhere are divots in the carpet of Bermuda, and the checkerboard is smeared where players have slid. "Can he just run out on the field," a father asks a gatekeeper. The plea gets a shrug at first, then a nod and a smile, and the boy races from the gate onto Neyland's hallowed turf. "All right," yells the beaming father to the son, "come back. You'll

yourself for a great season. Dismissed!" yells the band leader after one last feisty "Rocky Top" has been sung by fans and the courtly "Tennessee Waltz" has been played. The press moves in a gaggle of video and still cameras and microphones around the field in search of interviews. The

have to wait six years to do that again when you make the team." **The boy looks at the stadium around him, soaking up the moment, filled with awe to be standing where he is, knowing there's no better place on earth to be.**

coach kisses his daughters. The bold orange "T" fills the giant scoreboard, a glowing symbol of dominance. Players, coaches and fans linger, wishing to savor the moment.

"Lock it down, boys," yells a security guard as the last of the crowd trickles through the stadium tunnels to join the flood heading home. As the stadium grows quiet, the low

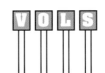

On a Hallowed hill in Tennessee
Like Beacon shining bright
The stately walls of old U.T.
Rise glorious to the sight.

So here's to you, old Tennessee
Our Alma Mater true,
We pledge to love and harmony
Our loyalty to you.

from the Tennessee Alma Mater, written in 1928 by Mary Fleming Meek

VOLS

TENNESSEE   MEMPHIS

QUARTER

DOWN

TO GO

BALL ON

T
TIME
OUTS

VISITOR
TIME
OUTS

three...two...one.

SIX!
DOWN
SSEE."

—John Ward, Tennessee play-by-play announcer from 1968 through 1998

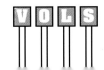

"Rocky Top," Tennessee's fight song since 1972

"GOOD OL' ROCKY TOP, ROCKY TOP TENNESSEE"

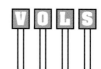

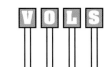

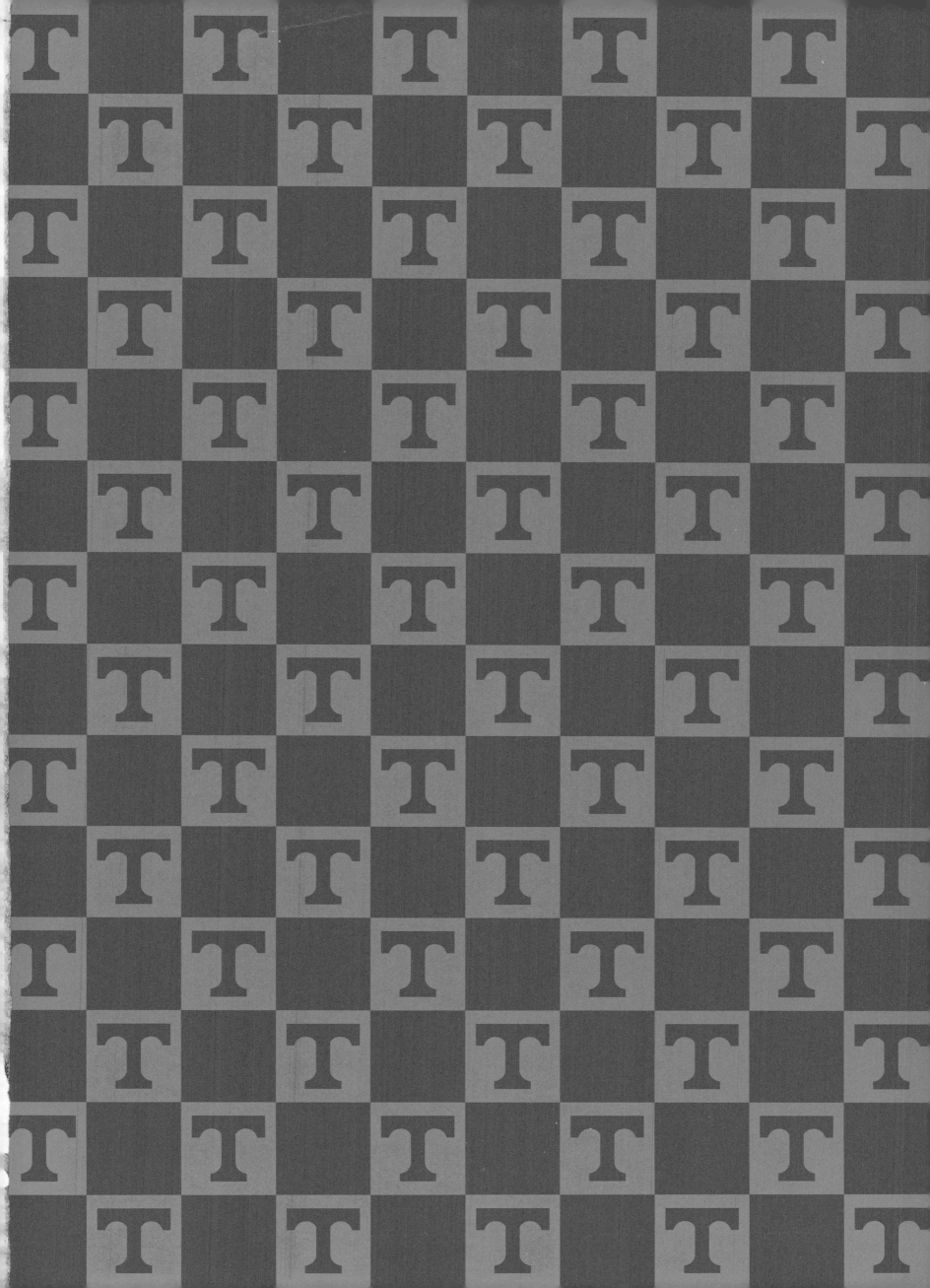

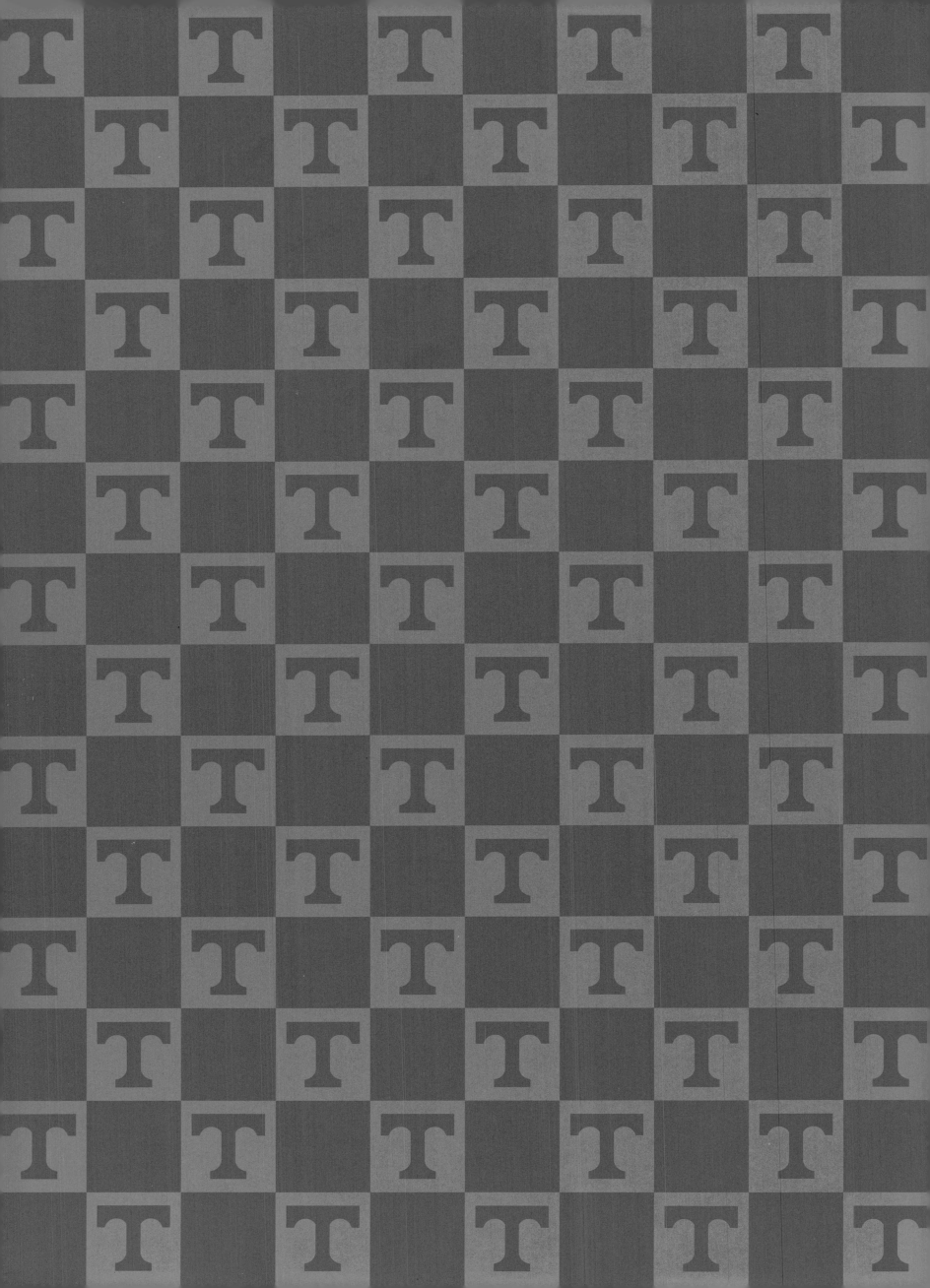